Alexander McLaren

The life of David as reflected in his Psalms

Alexander McLaren

The life of David as reflected in his Psalms

ISBN/EAN: 9783337101688

Printed in Europe, USA, Canada, Australia, Japan

Cover: Foto ©Lupo / pixelio.de

More available books at **www.hansebooks.com**

The following authors are expected to contribute to the HOUSEHOLD LIBRARY OF EXPOSITION:—

    The Rev. G. S. BARRETT, B.A., Norwich.
    The Rev. Professor A. B. BRUCE, D.D., Glasgow.
    The Rev. J. OSWALD DYKES, D.D., London.
    The Rev. DONALD FRASER, D.D., London.
    The Rev. WILLIAM GRAHAM, D.D., Liverpool.
    The Rev. JOHN LAIDLAW, D.D., Aberdeen
    The Rev. J. MARSHALL LANG, D.D., Glasgow.
    The Rev. ADOLPH SAPHIR, D.D., London.
    The Rev. CHARLES STANFORD, D.D., London.
    The Rev. WILLIAM FLEMING STEVENSON, M.A., Dublin.

Other names will be announced.

NEW YORK:
MACMILLAN & CO.

The Household Library of Exposition.

THE LIFE OF DAVID

AS REFLECTED IN HIS PSALMS.

THE LIFE OF DAVID

AS REFLECTED IN HIS PSALMS.

BY

ALEXANDER MACLAREN, D.D.

New York:
MACMILLAN & CO.
1880.

CONTENTS.

		PAGE
I.	INTRODUCTION,	1
II.	EARLY DAYS,	14
III.	EARLY DAYS—*continued*,	31
IV.	THE EXILE,	49
V.	THE EXILE—*continued*,	70
VI.	THE EXILE—*continued*,	86
VII.	THE EXILE—*continued*,	110
VIII.	THE EXILE—*continued*,	130
IX.	THE KING,	144
X.	THE KING—*continued*,	157
XI.	THE KING—*continued*,	174
XII.	THE KING—*continued*,	185
XIII.	THE TEARS OF THE PENITENT,	205
XIV.	CHASTISEMENTS,	232
XV.	THE SONGS OF THE FUGITIVE,	245

The Life of David as Reflected in his Psalms.

I.—INTRODUCTION.

PERHAPS the most striking characteristic of the life of David is its romantic variety of circumstances. What a many-coloured career that was which began amidst the pastoral solitudes of Bethlehem, and ended in the chamber where the dying ears heard the blare of the trumpets that announced the accession of Bathsheba's son! He passes through the most sharply contrasted conditions, and from each gathers some fresh fitness for his great work of giving voice and form to all the phases of devout feeling. The early shepherd life deeply influenced his character, and has left its traces on many a line of his psalms.

> "Love had he found in huts where poor men lie;
> His daily teachers had been woods and rills;
> The silence that is in the starry sky,
> The sleep that is among the lonely hills."

And then, in strange contrast with the meditative quiet and lowly duties of these first years, came the crowded vicissitudes of the tempestuous course through which he reached his throne —court minstrel, companion and friend of a king, idol of the people, champion of the armies of God—and in his sudden elevation keeping the gracious sweetness of his lowlier, and perhaps happier days. The scene changes with startling suddenness to the desert. He is "hunted like a partridge upon the mountains," a fugitive and half a freebooter, taking service at foreign courts, and lurking on the frontiers with a band of outlaws recruited from the "dangerous classes" of Israel. Like Dante and many more, he has to learn the weariness of the exile's lot—how hard his fare, how homeless his heart, how cold the courtesies of aliens, how unslumbering the suspicions which watch the refugee who fights on the side of his "natural enemies." One more swift transition and he is on the throne, for long years victorious, prosperous, and beloved.

> "Nor did he change ; but kept in lofty place
> The wisdom which adversity had bred,"

till suddenly he is plunged into the mire, and falsifies all his past, and ruins for ever, by the sin of his mature age, his peace of heart and the prosperity of his kingdom. Thenceforward trouble is never far away; and his later years are shaded with the saddening consciousness of his great fault, as well as by hatred and rebellion and murder in his family, and discontent and alienation in his kingdom.

None of the great men of Scripture pass through a course of so many changes; none of them touched human life at so many points; none of them were so tempered and polished by swift alternation of heat and cold, by such heavy blows and the friction of such rapid revolutions. Like his great Son and Lord, though in a lower sense, he, too, must be "in all points tempted like as we are," that his words may be fitted for the solace and strength of the whole world. Poets "learn in suffering what they teach in song." These quick transitions of fortune, and this wide experience, are the many-coloured threads from which the rich web of his psalms is woven.

And while the life is singularly varied, the character is also singularly full and versatile. In this respect, too, he is most unlike the other leading figures of Old Testament history. Contrast him, for example, with the stern majesty of Moses, austere and simple as the tables of stone; or with the unvarying tone in the gaunt strength of Elijah. These and the other mighty men in Israel are like the ruder instruments of music—the trumpet of Sinai, with its one prolonged note. David is like his own harp of many chords, through which the breath of God murmured, drawing forth wailing and rejoicing, the clear ring of triumphant trust, the low plaint of penitence, the blended harmonies of all devout emotions.

The man had his faults—grave enough. Let it be remembered that no one has judged them more rigorously than himself. The critics who have delighted to point at them have been anticipated by the penitent; and their indictment has been little more than the quotation of his own confession. His tremulously susceptible nature, especially assailable by the delights of sense, led him astray. There are traces in his life of occasional craft and untruthfulness which even the exigencies of exile and war do not wholly palliate. Flashes of fierce vengeance at times break from the clear sky of his generous nature. His strong affection became, in at least one case, weak and foolish fondness for an unworthy son.

But when all this is admitted, there remains a wonderfully rich, lovable character. He is the very ideal of a minstrel hero, such as the legends of the East especially love to paint. The shepherd's staff or sling, the sword, the sceptre, and the lyre are equally familiar to his hands. That union of the soldier and the poet gives the life a peculiar charm, and is very strikingly brought out in that chapter of the book of Samuel (2 Sam. xxiii.) which begins, "These be the last words of David," and after giving the swan-song of him whom it calls "the sweet psalmist of Israel," passes immediately to the other side of the dual character, with, "These be the names of the mighty men whom David had."

Thus, on the one side, we see the true poetic temperament, with all its capacities for keenest delight and sharpest agony, with its tremulous mobility, its openness to every impression, its gaze of child-like wonder, and eager welcome to whatsoever things are lovely, its simplicity and self-forgetfulness, its yearnings "after worlds half realized," its hunger for love, its pity, and its tears. He was made to be the inspired poet of the religious affections.

And, on the other side, we see the greatest qualities of a military leader of the antique type, in which personal daring and a strong arm count for more than strategic skill. He dashes at Goliath with an enthusiasm of youthful courage and faith. While still in the earliest bloom of his manhood, at the head of his wild band of outlaws, he shows himself sagacious, full of resource, prudent in counsel, and swift as lightning in act; frank and generous, bold and gentle, cheery in defeat, calm in peril, patient in privations and ready to share them with his men, modest and self-restrained in victory, chivalrous to his foes, ever watchful, ever hopeful—a born leader and king of men.

The basis of all was a profound, joyous trust in his Shepherd God, an ardour of personal love to Him, such as had never before been expressed, if it had ever found place, in Israel. That trust "opened his mouth to show forth" God's praise, and strengthened his "fingers to fight." He has told us himself what was his habitual temper, and how it was sustained: "I have set the Lord always before me. Because

He is at my right hand, I shall not be moved. Therefore my heart is glad, and my glory rejoiceth." (Psa. xvi. 8, 9.)

Thus endowed, he moved among men with that irresistible fascination which only the greatest exercise. From the day when he stole like a sunbeam into the darkened chamber where Saul wrestled with the evil spirit, he bows all hearts that come under his spell. The women of Israel chant his name with song and timbrel, the daughter of Saul confesses her love unasked, the noble soul of Jonathan cleaves to him, the rude outlaws in his little army peril their lives to gratify his longing for a draught from the well where he had watered his father's flocks; the priests let him take the consecrated bread, and trust him with Goliath's sword, from behind the altar; his lofty courtesy wins the heart of Abigail; the very king of the Philistines tells him that he is " good in his sight as an angel of God ;" the unhappy Saul's last word to him is a blessing; six hundred men of Gath forsake home and country to follow his fortunes when he returns from exile; and even in the dark close of his reign, though sin and self-indulgence, and neglect of his kingly duties, had weakened his subjects, loyalty, his flight before Absalom is brightened by instances of passionate devotion which no common character could have evoked; and even then his people are ready to die for him, and in their affectionate pride call him "the light of Israel." It was a prophetic instinct which made Jesse call his youngest boy by a name apparently before unused—David, "Beloved."

The Spirit of God, acting through these great natural gifts, and using this diversified experience of life, originated in him a new form of inspiration. The Law was the revelation of the mind, and, in some measure, of the heart, of God to man. The Psalm is the echo of the law, the return current set in motion by the outflow of the Divine will, the response of the heart of man to the manifested God. There had, indeed, been traces of hymns before David. There were the burst of triumph which the daughters of Israel sang, with timbrel and dance, over Pharaoh and his host; the prayer of Moses the man of God (Psa. xc.), so archaic in its tone, bearing in every line the impress of the weary wilderness and the law of death; the song of the dying lawgiver (Deut. xxxii.); the passionate pæan of Deborah; and some few briefer fragments. But, practically, the Psalm began with David; and though many hands struck the harp after him, even down at least to the return from exile, he remains emphatically "the sweet psalmist of Israel."

The psalms which are attributed to him have, on the whole, a marked similarity of manner. Their characteristics have been well summed up as "creative originality, predominantly elegiac tone, graceful form and movement, antique but lucid style;"* to which may be added the intensity of their devotion, the passion of Divine love that glows in them all. They correspond, too, with the circumstances of his life as given in the historical books. The early shepherd days, the manifold sorrows, the hunted wanderings, the royal authority, the wars, the triumphs, the sin, the remorse, which are woven together so strikingly in the latter, all reappear in the psalms. The illusions, indeed, are for the most part general rather than special, as is natural. His words are thereby the better fitted for ready application to the trials of other lives. But it has been perhaps too hastily assumed that the allusions are so general as to make it impossible

* Delitzsch, Kommentar, u. d. Psalter II. 376.

to connect them with any precise events, or to make the psalms and the history mutually illustrative. Much, no doubt, must be conjectured rather than affirmed, and much must be left undetermined; but when all deductions on that score have been made, it still appears possible to carry the process sufficiently far to gain fresh insight into the force and definiteness of many of David's words, and to use them with tolerable confidence as throwing light upon the narrative of his career. The attempt is made in some degree in this volume.

It will be necessary to prefix a few further remarks on the Davidic psalms in general. Can we tell which are David's? The Psalter, as is generally known, is divided into five books or parts, probably from some idea that it corresponded with the Pentateuch. These five books are marked by a doxology at the close of each, except the last. The first portion consists of Psa. i.—xli.; the second of Psa. xlii.—lxxii; the third of Psa. lxxiii.—lxxxix; the fourth of Psa. xc.—cvi.; and the fifth of Psa. cvii.—cl. The psalms attributed to David are unequally distributed through these five books. There are seventy-three in all, and they run thus :—In the first book there are thirty-seven; so that if we regard psalms i. and ii. as a kind of double introduction, a frontispiece and vignette title-page to the whole collection, the first book proper only two which are not regarded as David's. The second book has a much smaller proportion, only eighteen out of thirty-one. The third book has but one, the fourth two; while the fifth has fifteen, eight of which (cxxxviii.—cxlv.) occur almost at the close. The intention is obvious— to throw the Davidic psalms as much as possible together in the first two books. And the inference is not unnatural that these may have formed an earlier collection, to which were afterwards added the remaining three, with a considerable body of alleged psalms of David, which had subsequently come to light, placed side by side at the end, so as to round off the whole.

Be that as it may, one thing is clear from the arrangement of the Psalter, namely, that the superscriptions which give the authors' names are at least as old as the collection itself; for they have guided the order of the collection in the grouping not only of Davidic psalms, but also of those attributed to the sons of Korah (xlii.—xlix.) and to Asaph (lxxiii.—lxxxiii.)

The question of the reliableness of these superscriptions is hotly debated. The balance of modern opinion is decidedly against their genuineness. As in greater matters, so here "the higher criticism" comes to the consideration of their claims with a prejudice against them, and on very arbitrary grounds determines for itself, quite irrespective of these ancient voices, the date and authorship of the psalms. The extreme form of this tendency is to be found in the masterly work of Ewald, who has devoted all his vast power of criticism (and eked it out with all his equally great power of confident assertion) to the book, and has come to the conclusion that we have but eleven of David's psalms,—which is surely a result that may lead to questionings as to the method which has attained it.

These editorial notes are proved to be of extreme antiquity by such considerations as these: The Septuagint translators found them, and did not understand them; the synagogue preserves no traditions to explain them; the Book of Chronicles throws no light upon them; they are very rare in the two last books of the Psalter (Delitzsch, ii. 393). In some cases they are obviously erroneous, but in the greater number there is nothing inconsistent with their correctness in the psalms to which they are appended; while very frequently they throw a flood of light upon these, and all but prove their trustworthiness by their appropriateness. They are not authoritative, but they merit respectful consideration, and, as Dr Perowne puts it in his valuable work on the Psalms, stand on a par with the subscriptions to the Epistles in the New Testament. Regarding them thus, and yet examining the psalms to which they are prefixed, there seem to be about forty-five which we may attribute with some confidence to David, and with these we shall be concerned in this book.

II.—EARLY DAYS.

THE life of David is naturally divided into epochs, of which we may avail ourselves for the more ready arrangement of our material. These are—his early years up to his escape from the court of Saul, his exile, the prosperous beginning of his reign, his sin and penitence, his flight before Absalom's rebellion, and the darkened end.

We have but faint incidental traces of his life up to his anointing by Samuel, with which the narrative in the historical books opens. But perhaps the fact that the story begins with that consecration to office, is of more value than the missing biography of his childhood could have been. It teaches us the point of view from which Scripture regards its greatest names—as nothing, except in so far as they are God's instruments. Hence its carelessness, notwithstanding that so much of it is history, of all that merely illustrates the personal character of its heroes. Hence, too, the clearness with which, notwithstanding that indifference, the living men are set before us—the image cut with half a dozen strokes of the chisel.

We do not know the age of David when Samuel appeared in the little village with the horn of sacred oil in his hand. The only approximation to it is furnished by the fact, that he was thirty at the beginning of his reign. (2 Sam. v. 4.) If we take into account that his exile must have lasted for a very considerable period (one portion of it, his second flight to the Philistines, was sixteen months, 1 Sam. xxvii. 7),—that the previous residence at the court of Saul must have been long enough to give time for his gradual rise to popularity, and thereafter for the gradual development of the king's insane hatred,—that further back still there was an indefinite period, between the fight with Goliath, and the first visit as a minstrel-physician to the palace, which was spent at Bethlehem, and that that visit itself cannot have been very brief, since in its course he became very dear and familiar to Saul,—it will not seem that all these events could be crowded into less than some twelve or fifteen years, or that he could have been more than a lad of some sixteen years of age when Samuel's hand smoothed the sacred oil on his clustering curls.

How life had gone with him till then, we can easily gather from the narrative of Scripture. His father's household seems to have been one in which modest frugality ruled. There is no trace of Jesse having servants; his youngest child does menial work; the present which he sends to his king when David goes to court was simple, and such as a man in humble life would give—an ass load of bread, one skin of wine, and one kid—his flocks were small—" a few sheep." It would appear as if prosperity had not smiled on the family since the days of Jesse's grandfather, Boaz, that "mighty man of wealth." David's place in the household does not seem to have been a happy one. His father scarcely reckoned him amongst his sons, and answers Samuel's question, if the seven burly husbandmen whom he has seen are all his children, with a trace of contempt as he remembers that there is another, " and, behold, he keepeth the sheep." Of his mother we hear but once, and that incidentally, for a moment, long after. His brothers had no love for him, and do not appear to have shared either his heart or his fortunes. The boy evidently had the usual fate of souls like his, to grow up in uncongenial circumstances, little understood and less sympathised with by the common-place people round them, and thrown back therefore all the more decisively upon themselves. The process sours and spoils some, but it is the making of more—and where, as in this case, the nature is thrown back upon God, and not on its own morbid operation, strength comes from repression, and sweetness from endurance. He may have received some instruction in one of Samuel's schools for the prophets, but we are left in entire ignorance of what outward helps to unfold itself were given to his budding life.

Whatever others he had, no doubt those which are emphasized in the Bible story were the chief, namely, his occupation and the many gifts which it brought to him. The limbs, "like hinds' feet," the sinewy arms which "broke a bow of steel," the precision with which he used the sling, the agility which "leaped over a rampart," the health that glowed in his "ruddy" face, were the least of his obligations to the breezy uplands, where he kept his father's sheep.

His early life taught him courage, when he "smote the lion" and laid hold by his ugly muzzle of the bear that "rose against him," rearing itself upright for the fatal hug. Solitude and familiarity with nature helped to nurture the poetical side of his character, and to strengthen that meditative habit which blends so strangely with his impetuous activity, and which for the most part kept tumults and toils from invading his central soul. They threw him back on God who peopled the solitude and spoke in all nature. Besides this, he acquired in the sheepcote lessons which he practised on the throne, that rule means service, and that the shepherd of men holds his office in order that he may protect and guide. And in the lowly associations of his humble home, he learned the life of the people, their simple joys, their unconspicuous toils, their unnoticed sorrows—a priceless piece of knowledge both for the poet and for the king.

A breach in all the tranquil habits of this modest life was made by Samuel's astonishing errand. The story is told with wonderful picturesqueness and dramatic force. The minute account of the successive rejections of his brothers, Samuel's question and Jesse's answer, and then the pause of idle waiting till the messenger goes and returns, heighten the expectation with which we look for his appearance. And then what a sweet young face is lovingly painted for us! "He was ruddy, and withal of a beautiful countenance, and goodly to look to" (1 Sam. xvi. 12)—of fair complexion, with golden hair, which is rare among these swarthy, black-locked easterns, with lovely eyes (for that is the meaning of the words which the English Bible renders "of a beautiful countenance"), large and liquid as become a poet. So he stood before the old prophet, and with swelling heart and reverent awe received the holy chrism. In silence, as it would seem, Samuel anointed him. Whether the secret of his high destiny was imparted to him then, or left to be disclosed in future years, is not told. But at all events, whether with full understanding of what was before him or no, he must have been conscious of a call that would carry him far away from the pastures and olive yards of the little hamlet, and of a new Spirit stirring in him from that day forward.

This sudden change in all the outlook of his

life must have given new materials for thought when he went back to his humble task. Responsibility, or the prospect of it, makes lads into men very quickly. Graver meditations, humbler consciousness of weakness, a firmer trust in God who had laid the burden upon him, would do in days the work of years. And the necessity for bidding back the visions of the future in order to do faithfully the obscure duties of the present, would add self-control and patience, not usually the graces of youth. How swiftly he matured is singularly shown in the next recorded incident—his summons to the court of Saul, by the character of him drawn by the courtier who recommends him to the king. He speaks of David in words more suitable to a man of established renown than to a stripling. He is minstrel and warrior, "cunning in playing, and a mighty valiant man," and "skilled in speech (already eloquent), and fair in form, and the Lord is with him." (1 Sam. xvi. 18.) So quickly had the new circumstances and the energy of the Spirit of God, like tropical sunshine, ripened his soul.

That first visit to the court was but an episode in his life, however helpful to his growth it may have been. It would give him the knowledge of new scenes, widen his experience, and prepare him for the future. But it cannot have been of very long duration. Possibly his harp lost its power over Saul's gloomy spirit, when he had become familiar with its notes. For whatever reason, he returned to his father's house, and gladly exchanged the favour at court, which might have seemed to a merely ambitious man the first step towards fulfilling the prophecy of Samuel's anointing, for the freedom of the pastoral solitudes about Bethlehem. There he remained, living to outward seeming as in the quiet days before these two great earthquakes in his life, but with deeper thoughts and new power, with broader experience, and a wider horizon, until the hour when he was finally wrenched from his seclusion, and flung into the whirlpool of his public career.

There are none of David's psalms which can be with any certainty referred to this first period of his life; but it has left deep traces on many of them. The allusions to natural scenery and the frequent references to varying aspects of the shepherd's life are specimens of these. One characteristic of the poetic temperament is the faithful remembrance and cherishing of early days. How fondly he recalled them is shown in that most pathetic incident of his longing, as a weary exile, for one draught of water from the well at Bethlehem—where in the dear old times he had so often led his flocks.

But though we cannot say confidently that we have any psalms prior to his first exile, there are several which, whatever their date may be, are echoes of his thoughts in these first days. This is especially the case in regard to the group which describe varying aspects of nature —viz., Psalms xix., viii., xxix. They are unlike his later psalms in the almost entire absence of personal references, or of any trace of pressing cares, or of signs of a varied experience of human life. In their self-forgetful contemplation of nature, in their silence about sorrow, in their tranquil beauty, they resemble the youthful works of many a poet whose later verse throbs with quivering consciousness of life's agonies, or wrestles strongly with life's problems. They may not unnaturally be regarded as the outpouring of a young heart at leisure from itself, and from pain, far from men and very near God. The fresh mountain air of Bethlehem blows through them, and the dew of life's quiet morning is on them. The early experience supplied their materials, whatever was the date of their composition; and in them we can see what his inward life was in these budding years. The gaze of child-like wonder and awe upon the blazing brightness of the noonday, and on the mighty heaven with all its stars, the deep voice with which all creation spoke of God, the great thoughts of the dignity of man (thoughts ever welcome to lofty youthful souls), the gleaming of an inward light brighter than all suns, the consciousness of mysteries of weakness which may become miracles of sin in one's own heart, the assurance of close relation to God as His anointed and His servant, the cry for help and guidance—all this is what we should expect David to have thought and felt as he wandered among the hills, alone with God; and this is what these psalms give us.

Common to them all is the peculiar manner of looking upon nature, so uniform in David's psalms, so unlike more modern descriptive poetry. He can smite out a picture in a phrase, but he does not care to paint landscapes. He feels the deep analogies between man and his dwelling-place, but he does not care to lend to nature a shadowy life, the reflection of our own. Creation is to him neither a subject for poetical description, nor for scientific examination. It is nothing but the garment of God, the apocalypse of the heavenly. And common to them all is also the swift transition from the outward facts which reveal God, to the spiritual world, where His presence is, if it were possible, yet more needful, and His operations yet mightier. And common to them all is a certain rush of full thought and joyous power, which is again a characteristic of youthful work, and is unlike the elegiac tenderness and pathos of David's later hymns.

The nineteenth Psalm paints for us the glory of the heavens by day, as the eighth by night. The former gathers up the impressions of many a fresh morning when the solitary shepherd-boy watched the sun rising over the mountains of Moab, which close the eastern view from the hills above Bethlehem. The sacred silence of dawn, the deeper hush of night, have voice for his ear. "No speech! and no words! unheard is their voice." But yet, "in all the earth goeth forth their line,* and in the end of the habitable world their sayings." The heavens and the firmament, the linked chorus of day and night, are heralds of God's glory, with silent speech, heard in all lands, an unremitting voice. And as he looks, there leaps into the eastern heavens, not with the long twilight of northern lands, the sudden splendour, the sun radiant as a bridegroom from the bridal chamber, like some athlete impatient for the course. How the joy of morning and its new vigour throb in the words! And then he watches the strong runner climbing the heavens till the fierce heat beats down into the deep cleft of the Jordan, and all the treeless southern hills, as they slope towards the desert, lie bare and blazing beneath the beams.

The sudden transition from the revelation of God in nature to His voice in the law, has seemed to many critics unaccountable, except on the supposition that this psalm is made up of two fragments, put together by a later compiler; and some of them have even gone so far

---

* Their boundary, *i.e.*, their territory, or the region through which their witness extends. Others render "their chord," or sound (LXX. Ewald, etc.)

as to maintain that "the feeling which saw God revealed in the law did not arise till the time of Josiah." * But such a hypothesis is not required to explain either the sudden transition or the difference in style and rhythm between the two parts of the psalm, which unquestionably exists. The turn from the outer world to the better light of God's word, is most natural; the abruptness of it is artistic and impressive; the difference of style and measure gives emphasis to the contrast. There is also an obvious connection between the two parts, inasmuch as the law is described by epithets, which in part hint at its being a brighter sun, enlightening the eyes.

The Word which declares the will of the Lord is better than the heavens which tell His glory. The abundance of synonyms for that word show how familiar to his thoughts it was. To him it is "the law," "the testimonies" by which God witnesses of Himself and of man: "the statutes," the fixed settled ordinances; that which teaches "the fear of God," the "judgments" or utterances of His mind on human conduct. They are "perfect, firm, right, clean, pure,"—like that spotless sun—"eternal,

* "Psalms chronologically arranged"—following Ewald.

true." "They quicken, make wise, enlighten," even as the light of the lower world. His heart prizes them "more than gold," of which in his simple life he knew so little; more than "the honey," which he had often seen dropping from "the comb" in the pastures of the wilderness.

And then the twofold contemplation rises into the loftier region of prayer. He feels that there are dark depths in his soul, gloomier pits than any into which the noontide sun shines. He speaks as one who is conscious of dormant evils, which life has not yet evolved, and his prayer is more directed towards the future than the past, and is thus very unlike the tone of the later psalms, that wail out penitence and plead for pardon. "Errors," or weaknesses,—"faults" unknown to himself,—"high-handed sins,"*— such is the climax of the evils from which he prays for deliverance. He knows himself "Thy servant" (2 Sam. vii. 5, 8; Psa. lxxviii. 70)—an epithet which may refer to his consecration to God's work by Samuel's anointing. He needs not only a God who sets His glory in the

---

* The form of the word would make "reckless men" a more natural translation; but probably the context requires a third, more aggravated sort of sin.

heavens, nor even one whose will is made known, but one who will touch his spirit,—not merely a Maker, but a pardoning God; and his faith reaches its highest point as his song closes with the sacred name of the covenant Jehovah, repeated for the seventh time, and invoked in one final aspiration of a trustful heart, as "my Rock, and my Redeemer."

The eighth psalm is a companion picture, a night-piece, which, like the former, speaks of many an hour of lonely brooding below the heavens, whether its composition fall within this early period or no. The prophetic and doctrinal value of the psalms is not our main subject in the present volume, so that we have to touch but very lightly on this grand hymn. What does it show us of the singer? We see him, like other shepherds on the same hills, long after "keeping watch over his flocks by night," and overwhelmed by all the magnificence of an eastern sky, with its lambent lights. So bright, so changeless, so far,—how great they are, how small the boy that gazes up so wistfully. Are they gods, as all but his own nation believed? No,—" the work of Thy fingers," "which Thou hast ordained." The consciousness of God as their Maker delivers from the temptation of confounding bigness with greatness, and wakes into new energy that awful sense of personality which towers above all the stars. He is a babe and suckling—is that a trace of the early composition of the psalm?—still he knows that out of his lips, already beginning to break into song, and out of the lips of his fellows, God perfects praise. There speaks the sweet singer of Israel, prizing as the greatest of God's gifts his growing faculty, and counting his God-given words as nobler than the voice of "night unto night." God's fingers made these, but God's own breath is in him. God ordained them, but God visits him. The description of man's dignity and dominion indicates how familiar David was with the story in Genesis. It may perhaps also, besides all the large prophetic truths which it contains, have some special reference to his own earlier experience. It is at least worth noting that he speaks of the dignity of man as kingly, like that which was dawning on himself, and that the picture has no shadows either of sorrow or of sin,—a fact which may point to his younger days, when lofty thoughts of the greatness of the soul are ever natural and when in his case the afflictions and crimes that make their presence felt in all his later works had not fallen upon him. Perhaps, too, it may not be altogether fanciful to suppose that we may see the shepherd-boy surrounded by his flocks, and the wild creatures that prowled about the fold, and the birds asleep in their coverts beneath the moonlight, in his enumeration of the subjects of his first and happiest kingdom, where he ruled far away from men and sorrow, seeing God everywhere, and learning to perfect praise from his youthful lips.

III.—EARLY DAYS—*CONTINUED*.

IN addition to the psalms already considered, which are devoted to the devout contemplation of nature, and stand in close connection with David's early days, there still remains one universally admitted to be his. The twenty-ninth psalm, like both the preceding, has to do with the glory of God as revealed in the heavens, and with earth only as the recipient of skyey influences; but while these breathed the profoundest tranquillity, as they watched the silent splendour of the sun, and the peace of moonlight shed upon a sleeping world, this is all tumult and noise. It is a highly elaborate and vivid picture of a thunderstorm, such as must often have broken over the shepherd-psalmist as he crouched under some shelf of limestone, and gathered his trembling charge about him. Its very structure reproduces in sound an echo of the rolling peals reverberating among the hills.

There is first an invocation, in the highest strain of devout poetry, calling upon the "sons of God," the angels who dwell above the lower sky, and who see from above the slow gathering of the storm-clouds, to ascribe to Jehovah the glory of His name—His character as set forth in the tempest. They are to cast themselves before Him "in holy attire," as priests of the heavenly sanctuary. Their silent and expectant worship is like the brooding stillness before the storm. We feel the waiting hush in heaven and earth.

Then the tempest breaks. It crashes and leaps through the short sentences, each like the clap of the near thunder.

> *a.* The voice of Jehovah (is) on the waters.
> The God of glory thunders.
> *Jehovah (is) on many waters.*
> The voice of Jehovah in strength !
> The voice of Jehovah in majesty !
>
> *b.* The voice of Jehovah rending the cedars !
> *And Jehovah rends the cedars of Lebanon.*
> And makes them leap like a calf ;
> Lebanon and Sirion like a young buffalo.
> The voice of Jehovah hewing flashes of fire !
>
> *c.* The voice of Jehovah shakes the desert,
> *Jehovah shakes the Kadesh desert.*

> The voice of Jehovah makes the hinds writhe
> And scathes the woods—and in His temple—
> —All in it (are) saying, "Glory."

Seven times the roar shakes the world. The voice of the seven thunders is the voice of Jehovah. In the short clauses, with their uniform structure, the pause between, and the recurrence of the same initial words, we hear the successive peals, the silence that parts them, and the monotony of their unvaried sound. Thrice we have the reverberation rolling through the sky or among the hills, imitated by clauses which repeat previous ones, as indicated by the italics, and one forked flame blazes out in the brief, lightning-like sentence, "The voice of Jehovah (is) hewing flashes of fire," which wonderfully gives the impression of their streaming fiercely forth, as if cloven from some solid block of fire, their swift course, and their instantaneous extinction.

The range and effects of the storm, too, are vividly painted. It is first "on the waters," which may possibly mean the Mediterranean, but more probably, "the waters that are above the firmament," and so depicts the clouds as gathering high in air. Then it comes down with a crash on the northern mountains, splintering the gnarled cedars, and making Lebanon rock with all its woods—leaping across the deep valley of Cœlo-Syria, and smiting Hermon (for which Sirion is a Sidonian name), the crest of the Anti Lebanon, till it reels. Onward it sweeps—or rather, perhaps, it is all around the psalmist; and even while he hears the voice rolling from the furthest north, the extreme south echoes the roar. The awful voice shakes* the wilderness, as it booms across its level surface. As far south as Kadesh (probably Petra) the tremor spreads, and away in the forests of Edom the wild creatures in their terror slip their calves, and the oaks are scathed and stripped of their leafy honours. And all the while, like a mighty diapason sounding on through the tumult, the voice of the sons of God in the heavenly temple is heard proclaiming "Glory!"

The psalm closes with lofty words of confidence, built on the story of the past, as well as on the contemplation of the present. "Jehovah sat throned for (*i.e.*, to send on earth) the flood"

---

* Delitzsch would render "whirls in circles"— a picturesque allusion to the sand pillars which accompany storms in the desert.

which once drowned the world of old. "Jehovah will sit throned, a King for ever." That ancient judgment spoke of His power over all the forces of nature, in their most terrible form. So now and for ever, all are His servants, and effect His purposes. Then, as the tempest rolls away, spent and transient, the sunshine streams out anew from the softened blue over a freshened world, and every raindrop on the leaves twinkles into diamond light, and the end of the psalm is like the after brightness; and the tranquil low voice of its last words is like the songs of the birds again as the departing storm growls low and faint on the horizon. "The Lord will bless His people with peace."

Thus, then, nature spoke to this young heart. The silence was vocal; the darkness, bright; the tumult, order—and all was the revelation of a present God. It is told of one of our great writers that, when a child, he was found lying on a hill-side during a thunderstorm, and at each flash clapping his hands and shouting, unconscious of danger, and stirred to ecstasy. David, too, felt all the poetic elevation, and natural awe, in the presence of the crashing storm; but he felt something more. To him the thunder was not a power to tremble before, not a mere subject for poetic contemplation. Still less was it something, the like of which could be rubbed out of glass and silk, and which he had done with when he knew its laws. No increase of knowledge touching the laws of physical phenomena in the least affects the point of view which these Nature-psalms take. David said, " God makes and moves all things." We may be able to complete the sentence by a clause which tells something of the methods of His operation. But that is only a parenthesis after all, and the old truth remains widened, not overthrown by it. The psalmist knew that all being and action had their origin in God. He saw the last links of the chain, and knew that it was rivetted to the throne of God, though the intermediate links were unseen ; and even the fact that there were any was not present to his mind. We know something of these; but the first and the last of the series to him, are the first and the last to us also. To us as to him, the silent splendour of noonday speaks of God, and the nightly heavens pour the soft radiance of His "excellent name over all the earth." The tempest is His voice, and the wildest commotions in nature and among men break in obedient waves around His pillared throne.

> " Well roars the storm to those who hear
> A deeper voice across the storm ! "

There still remains one other psalm which may be used as illustrating the early life of David. The Twenty-third psalm is coloured throughout by the remembrances of his youthful occupation, even if its actual composition is of a later date. Some critics, indeed, think that the mention in the last verse of " the house of the Lord " compels the supposition of an origin subsequent to the building of the Temple ; but the phrase in question need not have anything to do with tabernacle or temple, and is most naturally accounted for by the preceding image of God as the Host who feasts His servants at His table. There are no other notes of time in the psalm, unless, with some commentators, we see an allusion in that image of the furnished table to the seasonable hospitality of the Gileadite chieftains during David's flight before Absalom (2 Sam. xvii. 27—29)—a reference which appears prosaic and flat. The absence of traces of distress and sorrow—so constantly present in the later songs—may be urged with some force in favour of the early date ; and if we follow one of the most valuable commentators (Hupfeld) in translating all the verbs as futures, and so make the whole a hymn of hope, we seem almost obliged to suppose that we have here the utterance of a youthful spirit, which ventured to look forward, because it first looked upward. In any case, the psalm is a transcript of thoughts that had been born and cherished in many a meditative hour among the lonely hills of Bethlehem. It is the echo of the shepherd life. We see in it the incessant care, the love to his helpless charge, which was expressed in and deepened by all his toil for them. He had to think for their simplicity, to fight for their defencelessness, to find their pasture, to guard them while they lay amid the fresh grass ; sometimes to use his staff in order to force their heedlessness with loving violence past tempting perils ; sometimes to guide them through gloomy gorges, where they huddled close at his heels ; sometimes to smite the lion and the bear that prowled about the fold—but all was for their good and meant their comfort. And thus he has learned, in preparation for his own kingdom, the inmost meaning of pre-eminence among men—and, more precious lesson still, thus he has learned the very heart of God. Long before, Jacob had spoken of Him as the "Shepherd of Israel;" but it was reserved for David to bring that sweet and wonderful name into closer relations with the single soul; and, with that peculiar enthusiasm of personal reliance, and recognition of God's love to the individual which stamps all his psalms, to say "The Lord is my Shepherd." These dumb companions of his, in their docility to his guidance, and absolute trust in his care, had taught him the secret of peace in helplessness, of patience in ignorance. The green strips of meadow-land where the clear waters brought life, the wearied flocks sheltered from the mid-day heat, the quiet course of the little stream, the refreshment of the sheep by rest and pasture, the smooth paths which he tried to choose for them, the rocky defiles through which they had to pass, the rod in his hand that guided, and chastised, and defended, and was never lifted in anger,—all these, the familiar sights of his youth, pass before us as we read; and to us too, in our widely different social state, have become the undying emblems of the highest care and the wisest love. The psalm witnesses how close to the youthful heart the consciousness of God must have been, which could thus transform and glorify the little things which were so familiar. We can feel, in a kind of lazy play of sentiment, the fitness of the shepherd's life to suggest thoughts of God—because it is not our life. But it needs both a meditative habit and a devout heart, to feel that the trivialities of our own daily tasks speak to us of Him. The heavens touch the earth on the horizon of our vision, but it always seems furthest to the sky from the spot where we stand. To the psalmist, however,—as in higher ways to his Son and Lord,—all things around him were full of God; and as the majesties of nature, so the trivialities of man's works—shepherds and fishermen—were solemn with deep meanings and shadows of the heavenly. With such lofty thoughts he fed his youth.

The psalm, too, breathes the very spirit of sunny confidence and of perfect rest in God. We have referred to the absence of traces of sorrow, and to the predominant tone of hopefulness, as possibly favouring the supposition of an early origin. But it matters little whether they were young eyes which looked so courageously into the unknown future, or whether we have here the more solemn and weighty hopes of age, which can have few hopes at all, unless they be rooted in God. The spirit expressed in the psalm is so thoroughly David's, that in his younger days, before it was worn with responsibilities and sorrows, it must have been especially strong. We may therefore fairly take the tone of this song of the Shepherd God as expressing the characteristic of his godliness in the happy early years. In his solitude he was glad. One happy thought fills the spirit; one simple emotion thrills the chords of his harp. No doubts, or griefs, or remorse throw their shadows upon him. He is conscious of dependence, but he is above want and fear. He does not ask, he has—he possesses God, and is at rest in Him. He is satisfied with that fruition which blesseth all who hunger for God, and is the highest form of communion with Him. As the present has no longings, the future has no terrors. All the horizon is clear, all the winds are still, the ocean at rest, "and birds of peace sit brooding on the charmed wave." If there be foes, God holds them back. If there lie far off among the hills any valley of darkness, its black portals cast no gloom over him, and will not when he enters. God is his Shepherd, and, by another image, God is his Host. The life which in one aspect, by reason of its continual change, and occupation with outward things, may be compared to the journeyings of a flock, is in another aspect, by reason of its inward union with the stability of God, like sitting ever at the table which His hand has spread as for a royal banquet, where the oil of gladness glistens on every head, and the full cup of Divine pleasure is in every hand. For all the outward and pilgrimage aspect, the psalmist knows that only Goodness and Mercy —these two white-robed messengers of God— will follow his steps, however long may be the term of the days of his yet young life; for all the inward, he is sure that, in calm, unbroken fellowship, he will dwell in the house of God, and that when the twin angels who fed and guided him all his young life long have finished their charge, and the days of his journeyings are ended, there stretches beyond a still closer union with his heavenly Friend, which will be perfected in His true house "for ever." We look in vain for another example, even in David's psalms, of such perfect, restful trust in God. These clear notes are perhaps the purest utterance ever given of "the peace of God which passeth all understanding."

Such were the thoughts and hopes of the lad who kept his father's sheep at Bethlehem. He lived a life of lofty thoughts and lowly duties. He heard the voice of God amidst the silence of the hills, and the earliest notes of his harp echoed the deep tones. He learned courage as well as tenderness from his daily tasks, and patience from the contrast between them and the high vocation which Samuel's mysterious anointing had opened before him. If we remember how disturbing an influence the consciousness of it might have wrought in a soul less filled with God, we may perhaps accept as probably correct the superscription which refers one sweet, simple psalm to him, and may venture to suppose that it expresses the contentment, undazzled by visions of coming greatness, that calmed his heart. "Lord, my heart is not haughty, nor mine eyes lofty; neither do I exercise myself in great matters, or in things too high for me. Surely I have smoothed and quieted my soul: like a weanling on his mother's (breast), like a weanling is my soul within me." (Psa. cxxxi.) So lying in God's arms, and content to be folded in His embrace, without seeking anything beyond, he is tranquil in his lowly lot.

It does not fall within our province to follow the course of the familiar narrative through the picturesque events that led him to fame and position at court. The double character of minstrel and warrior, to which we have already referred, is remarkably brought out in his double introduction to Saul, once as soothing the king's gloomy spirit with the harmonies of his shepherd's harp, once as bringing down the boasting giant of Gath with his shepherd's sling. On the first occasion his residence in the palace seems to have been ended by Saul's temporary recovery. He returns to Bethlehem for an indefinite time, and then leaves it and all its peaceful tasks for ever. The dramatic story of the duel with Goliath needs no second telling. His arrival at the very crisis of the war, the eager courage with which he leaves his baggage in the hands of the guard and runs down the valley to the ranks of the army, the busy hum of talk among the Israelites, the rankling jealousy of his brother that curdles into bitter jeers, the modest courage with which he offers himself as champion, the youthful enthusiasm of brave trust in "the Lord, that delivered me out of the paw of the lion, and out of the paw of the bear;" the wonderfully vivid picture of the young hero with his shepherd staff in one hand, his sling in the other, and the rude wallet by his side, which had carried his simple meal, and now held the smooth stone from the brook that ran between the armies in the bottom of the little valley— the blustering braggadocio of the big champion, the boy's devout confidence in "the name of the Lord of hosts;" the swift brevity of the narrative of the actual fight, which in its hurrying clauses seems to reproduce the light-footed eagerness of the young champion, or the rapid whizz of the stone ere it crashed into the thick forehead; the prostrate bulk of the dead giant prone upon the earth, and the conqueror, slight and agile, hewing off the huge head with Goliath's own useless sword;—all these incidents, so full of character, so antique in manner, so weighty with lessons of the impotence of strength that is merely material, and the powe of a living enthusiasm of faith in God, may, for our present purposes, be passed with a mere glance. One observation may, however, be allowed. After the victory, Saul is represented as not knowing who David was, and as sending Abner to find out where he comes from. Abner, too, professes entire ignorance; and when David appears before the king, "with the head of the Philistine in his hand," he is asked, "Whose son art thou, young man?" It has been thought that here we have an irreconcilable contradiction with previous narratives, according to which there was close intimacy between him and the king, who "loved him greatly," and gave him an office of trust about his person. Suppositions of "dislocation of the narrative," the careless adoption by the compiler of two separate legends, and the like, have been freely indulged in. But it may at least be suggested as a possible explanation of the seeming discrepancy, that when Saul had passed out of his moody madness it is not wonderful that he should have forgotten all which had occurred in his paroxysm. It is surely a common enough psychological phenomenon that a man restored to sanity has no remembrance of the events during his mental aberration. And as for Abner's profession of ignorance, an incipient jealousy of this stripling hero may naturally have made the "captain of the host" willing to keep the king as ignorant as he could concerning a probable formidable rival. There is no need to suppose he was really ignorant, but only that it suited him to say that he was.

With this earliest deed of heroism the peaceful private days are closed, and a new epoch of court favour and growing popularity begins. The impression which the whole story leaves upon one is well summed up in a psalm which the Septuagint adds to the Psalter. It is not found in the Hebrew, and has no pretension to be David's work; but, as a *résumé* of the salient points of his early life, it may fitly end our considerations of this first epoch.

"This is the autograph psalm of David, and beyond the number (*i.e.*, of the psalms in the Psalter), when he fought the single fight with Goliath :—

"(1.) I was little among my brethren, and the youngest in the house of my father: I kept the flock of my father. (2.) My hands made a pipe, my fingers tuned a psaltery. (3.) And who shall tell it to my Lord? He is the Lord, He shall hear me. (4.) He sent His angel (messenger), and took me from the flocks of my father, and anointed me with the oil of His anointing. (5.) But my brethren were fair and large, and in them the Lord took not pleasure. (6.) I went out to meet the Philistine, and he cursed me by his idols. (7.) But I, drawing his sword, beheaded him, and took away reproach from the children of Israel."

IV.—THE EXILE.

DAVID'S first years at the court of Saul in Gibeah do not appear to have produced any psalms which still survive.

> "The sweetest songs are those
> Which tell of saddest thought."

It was natural, then, that a period full of novelty and of prosperous activity, very unlike the quiet days at Bethlehem, should rather accumulate materials for future use than be fruitful in actual production. The old life shut to behind him for ever, like some enchanted door in a hillside, and an unexplored land lay beckoning before. The new was widening his experience, but it had to be mastered, to be assimilated by meditation before it became vocal.

The bare facts of this section are familiar and soon told. There is first a period in which he is trusted by Saul, who sets him in high command, with the approbation not only of the people, but even of the official classes. But a new dynasty resting on military pre-eminence cannot afford to let a successful soldier stand on the steps of the throne; and the shrill chant of the women out of all the cities of Israel, which even in Saul's hearing answered the praises of his prowess with a louder acclaim for David's victories, startled the king for the first time with a revelation of the national feeling. His unslumbering suspicion "eyed David from that day." Rage and terror threw him again into the gripe of his evil spirit, and in his paroxysm he flings his heavy spear, the symbol of his royalty, at the lithe harper, with fierce vows of murder. The failure of his attempt to kill David seems to have aggravated his dread of him as bearing a charm which won all hearts and averted all dangers. A second stage is marked not only by Saul's growing fear, but by David's new position. He is removed from court, and put in a subordinate command, which only extends his popularity, and brings him into more immediate contact with the mass of the people. "All Israel and Judah loved David, because he went out and came in before them." Then follows the offer of Saul's elder daughter in marriage, in the hope that by playing upon his gratitude and his religious feeling, he might be urged to some piece of rash bravery that would end him without scandal. Some new caprice of Saul's, however, leads him to insult David by breaking his pledge at the last moment, and giving the promised bride to another. Jonathan's heart was not the only one in Saul's household that yielded to his spell. The younger Michal had been cherishing his image in secret, and now tells her love. Her father returns to his original purpose, with the strange mixture of tenacity and capricious changefulness that marks his character, and again attempts, by demanding a grotesquely savage dowry, to secure David's destruction. But that scheme, too, fails; and he becomes a member of the royal house.

This third stage is marked by Saul's deepening panic hatred, which has now become a fixed idea. All his attempts have only strengthened David's position, and he looks on his irresistible advance with a nameless awe. He calls, with a madman's folly, on Jonathan and on all his servants to kill him; and then, when his son appeals to him, his old better nature comes over him, and with a great oath he vows that David shall not be slain. For a short time David returns to Gibeah, and resumes his former relations with Saul, but a new victory over the Philistines rouses the slumbering jealousy. Again the "evil spirit" is upon him, and the great javelin is flung with blind fury, and sticks quivering in the wall. It is night, and David flies to his house. A stealthy band of assassins from the palace surround the house with orders to prevent all egress, and, by what may be either the strange whim of a madman, or the cynical shamelessness of a tyrant, to slay him in the open daylight. Michal, who, though in after time she showed a strain of her father's proud godlessness, and an utter incapacity of understanding the noblest parts of her husband's character, seems to have been a true wife in these early days, discovers, perhaps with a woman's quick eye sharpened by love, the crouching murderers, and with rapid promptitude urges immediate flight. Her hands let him down from the window—the house being probably on the wall. Her ready wit dresses up one of those mysterious teraphim (which appear to have had some connection with idolatry or magic, and which are strange pieces of furniture for David's house), and lays it in the bed to deceive the messengers, and so gain a little more time before pursuit began. "So David fled and escaped, and came to Samuel to Ramah," and thus ended his life at court.

Glancing over this narrative, one or two points come prominently forth. The worth of these events to David must have lain chiefly in the abundant additions made to his experience of life, which ripened his nature, and developed new powers. The meditative life of the sheep-fold is followed by the crowded court and camp. Strenuous work, familiarity with men, constant vicissitude, take the place of placid thought, of calm seclusion, of tranquil days that knew no changes but the alternation of sun and stars, storm and brightness, green pastures and dusty paths. He learned the real world, with its hate and effort, its hollow fame and its whispering calumnies. Many illusions no doubt faded, but the light that had shone in his solitude still burned before him for his guide, and a deeper trust in his Shepherd God was rooted in his soul by all the shocks of varying fortune. The passage from the visions of youth and the solitary resolves of early and uninterrupted piety to the naked realities of a wicked world, and the stern self-control of manly godliness, is ever painful and perilous. Thank God! it may be made clear gain, as it was by this young hero psalmist.

David's calm indifference to outward circumstances affecting himself, is very strikingly expressed in his conduct. Partly from his poetic temperament, partly from his sweet natural unselfishness, and chiefly from his living trust in God, he accepts whatever happens with equanimity, and makes no effort to alter it. He originates nothing. Prosperity comes unsought, and dangers unfeared. He does not ask for Jonathan's love, or the people's favour, or the women's songs, or Saul's daughter. If Saul gives him command he takes it, and does his work. If Saul flings his javelin at him, he simply springs aside and lets it whizz past. If his high position is taken from him, he is quite content with a lower. If a royal alliance is offered, he accepts it; if it is withdrawn, he is not ruffled; if renewed, he is still willing. If a busy web of intrigue is woven round him, he takes no notice. If reconciliation is proposed, he cheerfully goes back to the palace. If his life is threatened he goes home. He will not stir to escape but for the urgency of his wife. So well had he already begun to learn the worthlessness of life's trifles. So thoroughly does he practice his own precept, "Fret not thyself because of evil-doers;" "rest in the Lord, and wait patiently for Him." (Psa. xxxvii. 1, 7.)

This section gives also a remarkable impression of the irresistible growth of his popularity and influence. The silent energy of the Divine purpose presses his fortunes onward with a motion slow and inevitable as that of a glacier. The steadfast flow circles unchecked round, or rises victorious over all hindrances. Efforts to ruin, to degrade, to kill—one and all fail. Terror and hate, suspicion and jealousy, only bring him nearer the goal. A clause which comes in thrice in the course of one chapter, expresses this fated advance. In the first stage of his court life, we read, "David prospered" (1 Sam. xviii. 5, margin), and again with increased emphasis it is told as the result of the efforts to crush him, that, "He prospered in all his ways, and the Lord was with him" (verse 14), and yet again, in spite of Saul's having "become his enemy continually," he "prospered more than all the servants of Saul" (verse 30).

He moves onward as stars in their courses move, obeying the equable impulse of the calm and conquering will of God.

The familiar Scripture antithesis, which naturally finds its clearest utterance in the words of the last inspired writer—namely, the eternal opposition of Light and Darkness, Love and Hate, Life and Death, is brought into sharpest relief by the juxtaposition and contrast of David and Saul. This is the key to the story. The two men are not more unlike in person than in spirit. We think of the one with his ruddy beauty and changeful eyes, and lithe slight form, and of the other gaunt and black, his giant strength weakened, and his "goodly" face scarred with the lightnings of his passions—and as they look so they are. The one full of joyous energy, the other devoured by gloom; the one going in and out among the people and winning universal love, the other sitting moody and self-absorbed behind his palace walls; the one bringing sweet clear tones of trustful praise from his harp, the other shaking his huge spear in his madness; the one ready for action and prosperous in it all, the other paralyzed, shrinking from all work, and leaving the conduct of the war to the servant whom he feared; the one conscious of the Divine presence making him strong and calm, the other writhing in the gripe of his evil spirit, and either foaming in fury, or stiffened into torpor; the one steadily growing in power and favour with God and man, the other sinking in deeper mire, and wrapped about with thickening mists as he moves to his doom. The tragic pathos of these two lives in their fateful antagonism is the embodiment of that awful alternative of life and death, blessing and cursing, which it was the very aim of Judaism to stamp ineffaceably on the conscience.

David's flight begins a period to which a large number of his psalms are referred. We may call them "The Songs of the Outlaw." The titles in the psalter connect several with specific events during his persecution by Saul, and besides these, there are others which have marked characteristics in common, and may therefore be regarded as belonging to the same time. The bulk of the former class are found in the second book of the psalter (Ps. xlii.—lxxii.), which has been arranged with some care. There are first eight Korahite psalms, and one of

Asaph's; then a group of fifteen Davidic (li.—lxv.), followed by two anonymous; then three more of David's (lxviii.—lxx.), followed by one anonymous and the well-known prayer "for Solomon." Now it is worth notice that the group of fifteen psalms ascribed to David is as nearly as possible divided in halves, eight having inscriptions which give a specific date of composition, and seven having no such detail. There has also been some attempt at arranging the psalms of these two classes alternately, but that has not been accurately carried out. These facts show that the titles are at all events as old as the compilation of the second book of the psalter, and were regarded as accurate then. Several points about the complete book of psalms as we have it, seem to indicate that these two first books were an older nucleus, which was in existence long prior to the present collection —and if so, the date of the titles must be carried back a very long way indeed, and with a proportionate increase of authority.

Of the eight psalms in the second book having titles with specific dates, five (Ps. lii., liv., lvi., lvii., lix.) are assigned to the period of the Sauline persecution, and, as it would appear, with accuracy. There is a general similarity of tone in them all, as well as considerable parallelisms of expression, favourite phrases and metaphors, which are favourable to the hypothesis of a nearly cotemporaneous date. They are all in what, to use a phrase from another art, we may call David's earlier manner. For instance, in all the psalmist is surrounded by enemies. They would "swallow him up" (lvi. 1, 2; lvii. 3). They "oppress" him (liv. 3; lvi. 1). One of their weapons is calumny, which seems from the frequent references to have much moved the psalmist. Their tongues are razors (lii. 2), or swords (lvii. 4; lix. 7; lxiv. 3). They seem to him like crouching beasts ready to spring upon harmless prey (lvi. 6; lvii. 6; lix. 3); they are "lions" (lvii. 4), dogs (lix. 6, 14). He is conscious of nothing which he has done to provoke this storm of hatred (lix. 3; lxiv. 4.) The "strength" of God is his hope (liv. 1; lix. 9, 17). He is sure that retribution will fall upon the enemies (lii. 5; liv. 5; lvi. 7; lvii. 6; lix. 8—15; lxiv. 7, 8). He vows and knows that psalms of deliverance will yet succeed these plaintive cries (lii. 9; liv. 7; lvi. 12; lvii. 7—11; lix. 16, 17).

We also find a considerable number of psalms in the first book of the psalter which present the same features, and may therefore probably be classed with these as belonging to the time of his exile. Such for instance are the seventh and thirty-fourth, which have both inscriptions referring them to this period, with others which we shall have to consider presently. The imagery of the preceding group reappears in them. His enemies are lions (vii. 2; xvii. 12; (xxii. 13; xxxv. 17); dogs (xxii. 16); bulls xxii. 12). Pitfalls and snares are in his path (vii. 15; xxxi. 4; xxxv. 7). He passionately protests his innocence, and the kindliness of his heart to his wanton foes (vii. 3—5; xvii. 3, 4); whom he has helped and sorrowed over in their sickness (xxxv. 13, 14)—a reference, perhaps, to his solacing Saul in his paroxysms with the music of his harp. He dwells on retribution with vehemence (vii. 11—16; xi. 5—7; xxxi. 23; xxxv. 8), and on his own deliverance with confidence.

These general characteristics accurately correspond with the circumstances of David during the years of his wanderings. The scenery and life of the desert colours the metaphors which describe his enemies as wild beasts; himself as a poor hunted creature amongst pits and snares; or as a timid bird flying to the safe crags, and God as his Rock. Their strong assertions of innocence accord with the historical indications of Saul's gratuitous hatred, and appear to distinguish the psalms of this period from those of Absalom's revolt, in which the remembrance of his great sin was too deep to permit of any such claims. In like manner the prophecies of the enemies' destruction are too triumphant to suit that later time of exile, when the father's heart yearned with misplaced tenderness over his worthless son, and nearly broke with unkingly sorrow for the rebel's death. Their confidence in God, too, has in it a ring of joyousness in peril which corresponds with the buoyant faith that went with him through all the desperate adventures and hairbreadth escapes of the Sauline persecution. If then we may, with some confidence, read these psalms in connection with that period, what a noble portraiture of a brave, devout soul looks out upon us from them. We see him in the first flush of his manhood—somewhere about five-and-twenty years old—fronting perils of which he is fully conscious, with calm strength and an enthusiasm of trust that lifts his spirit above them all, into a region of fellowship with God which no tumult can invade, and which no remembrance of black transgression troubled and stained. His harp is his solace in his wanderings; and while plaintive notes are flung from its strings, as is needful for the deepest harmonies of praise here, every wailing tone melts into clear ringing notes of glad affiance in the " God of his mercy."

Distinct references to the specific events of his wanderings are, undoubtedly, rare in them, though even these are more obvious than has been sometimes carelessly assumed. Their infrequency and comparative vagueness has been alleged against the accuracy of the inscriptions which allocate certain psalms to particular occasions. But in so far as it is true that these allusions are rare and inexact, the fact is surely rather in favour of than against the correctness of the titles. For if these are not suggested by obvious references in the psalms to which they are affixed, by what can they have been suggested but by a tradition considerably older than the compilation of the psalter? Besides, the analogy of all other poetry would lead us to expect precisely what we find in these psalms —general and not detailed allusions to the writer's circumstances. The poetic imagination does not reproduce the bald prosaic facts which have set it in motion, but the echo of them broken up and etherealised. It broods over them till life stirs, and the winged creature bursts from them to sing and soar.

If we accept the title as accurate, the fifty-ninth psalm is the first of these Songs of the Outlaw. It refers to the time "when Saul sent, and they watched the house to kill him." Those critics who reject this date, which they do on very weak grounds, lose themselves in a chaos of assumptions as to the occasion of the psalm. The Chaldean invasion, the assaults in the time of Nehemiah, and the era of the Maccabees, are alleged with equal confidence and equal groundlessness. "We believe that it is most advisable to adhere to the title, and most scientific to ignore these hypotheses built on nothing." (Delitzsch.)

It is a devotional and poetic commentary on the story in Samuel. There we get the bare facts of the assassins prowling by night round David's house; of Michal's warning; of her ready-witted trick to gain time, and of his hasty flight to Samuel at Ramah. In the narrative David is, as usual at this period, passive and silent; but when we turn to the psalm, we learn the tone of his mind as the peril bursts upon him, and all the vulgar craft and fear fades from before his lofty enthusiasm of faith.

The psalm begins abruptly with a passionate cry for help, which is repeated four times, thus bringing most vividly before us the extremity of the danger and the persistency of the suppliant's trust. The peculiar tenderness and closeness of his relation to his heavenly Friend, which is so characteristic of David's psalms, and which they were almost the first to express, breathes through the name by which he invokes help, "my God." The enemies are painted in words which accurately correspond with the history, and which by their variety reveal how formidable they were to the psalmist. They "lie in wait (literally weave plots) for my life." They are "workers of iniquity," "men of blood," insolent or violent ("mighty" in English version). He asserts his innocence, as ever in these Sauline psalms, and appeals to God in confirmation, "not for my transgressions, nor for my sins, O Lord." He sees these eager tools of royal malice hurrying to their congenial work: "they run and prepare themselves." And then, rising high above all encompassing evils, he grasps at the throne of God in a cry, which gains additional force when we remember that the would-be murderers compassed his house in the night. "Awake to meet me, and behold;" as if he had said, "In the darkness do Thou see; at midnight sleep not Thou." The prayer is continued in words which heap together with unwonted abundance the Divine names, in each of which lie an appeal to God and a pillar of faith. As Jehovah, the self-existent Fountain of timeless Being; as the God of Hosts, the Commander of all the embattled powers of the universe, whether they be spiritual or material; as the GOD of Israel, who calls that people His, and has become theirs—he stirs up the strength of God to "awake to visit all the heathen,"—a prayer which has been supposed to compel the reference of the whole psalm to the assaults of Gentile nations, but which may be taken as an anticipation on David's lips of the truth that, "They are not all Israel which are of Israel." After a terrible petition—"Be not merciful to any secret plotters of evil "—there is a pause (Selah) to be filled, as it would appear, by some chords on the harp, or the blare of the trumpets, thus giving time to dwell on the previous petitions.

But still the thought of the foe haunts him, and he falls again to the lower level of painting their assembling round his house, and their whispers as they take their stand. It would appear that the watch had been kept up for more than one night. How he flings his growing scorn of them into the sarcastic words, "They return at evening; they growl like a dog, and compass the city" (or "go their rounds in the city"). One sees them stealing through the darkness, like the troops of vicious curs that infest Eastern cities, and hears their smothered threatenings as they crouch in the shadow of the unlighted streets. Then growing bolder, as the night deepens and sleep falls on the silent houses: "Behold they pour out with their mouth, swords (are) in their lips, for 'who hears'?" In magnificent contrast with these skulking murderers fancying themselves unseen and unheard, David's faith rends the heaven, and, with a daring image which is copied in a much later psalm (ii. 4), shows God gazing on them with Divine scorn which breaks in laughter and mockery. A brief verse, which recurs at the end of the psalm, closes the first portion of the psalm with a calm expression of untroubled trust, in beautiful contrast with the peril and tumult of soul, out of which it rises steadfast and ethereal, like a rainbow spanning a cataract. A slight error appears to have crept into the Hebrew text, which can be easily corrected from the parallel verse at the end; and then the quiet confident words are—

" My strength ! upon Thee will I wait,
For God is my fortress ! "

The second portion is an intensification of the first; pouring out a terrible prayer for exemplary retribution on his enemies; asking that no speedy destruction may befall them, but that God would first of all "make them reel" by the blow of His might; would then fling them prostrate; would make their pride and fierce words a net to snare them; and then, at last, would bring them to nothing in the hot flames of His wrath—that the world may know that He is king. The picture of the prowling dogs recurs with deepened scorn and firmer confidence that they will hunt for their prey in vain.

> "And they return at evening; they growl like a dog,
> And compass the city.
> They—they prowl about for food
> If (or, since) they are not satisfied, they spend the night (in the search.)"

There is almost a smile on his face as he thinks of their hunting about for him, like hungry hounds snuffing for their meal in the kennels, and growling now in disappointment—while he is safe beyond their reach. And the psalm ends with a glad burst of confidence, and a vow of praise very characteristic on his lips—

> "But I—I will sing Thy power,
> And shout aloud, in the morning, Thy mercy,
> For Thou hast been a fortress for me.
> And a refuge in the day of my trouble.
> My strength! unto Thee will I harp,
> For God is my fortress—the God of my mercy."

Thrice he repeats the vow of praise. His harp was his companion in his flight, and even in the midst of peril the poet's nature appears which regards all life as materials for song, and the devout spirit appears which regards all trial as occasions for praise. He has calmed his own spirit, as he had done Saul's, by his song, and by prayer has swung himself clear above fightings and fears. The refrain, which occurs twice in the psalm, witnesses to the growth of his faith even while he sings. At first he could only say in patient expectance, "My strength! I will wait upon thee, for God is my fortress." But at the end his mood is higher, his soul has caught fire as it revolves, and his last words are a triumphant amplification of his earlier trust: "My strength! unto thee will I sing with the harp—for God is my fortress—the God of my mercy."

V.—THE EXILE—*CONTINUED.*

"SO David fled, and escaped and came to Samuel to Ramah, and told him all that Saul had done unto him. And he and Samuel went and dwelt in Naioth" (1 Sam. xix. 18)—or, as the word probably means, in the collection of students' dwellings, inhabited by the sons of the prophets, where possibly there may have been some kind of right of sanctuary. Driven thence by Saul's following him, and having had one last sorrowful hour of Jonathan's companionship—the last but one on earth—he fled to Nob, whither the ark had been carried after the destruction of Shiloh. The story of his flight had not reached the solitary little town among the hills, and he is received with the honour due to the king's son-in-law. He pleads urgent secret business for Saul as a reason for his appearance with a slender retinue, and unarmed; and the priest, after some feeble scruples, supplies the handful of hungry fugitives with the shewbread. But David's quick eye caught a swarthy face peering at him from some enclosure of the simple forest sanctuary, and as he recognised Doeg the Edomite, Saul's savage herdsman, a cold foreboding of evil crept over his heart, and made him demand arms from the peaceful priest. The lonely tabernacle was guarded by its own sanctity, and no weapons were there, except one trophy which was of good omen to David—Goliath's sword. He eagerly accepts the matchless weapon which his hand had clutched on that day of danger and deliverance, and thus armed, lest Doeg should try to bar his flight, he hurries from the pursuit which he knew that the Edomite's malignant tongue would soon bring after him. The tragical end of the unsuspecting priest's kindness brings out the furious irrational suspicion and cruelty of Saul. He rages at his servants as leagued with David in words which have a most dreary sound of utter loneliness sighing through all their fierce folly: "All of you have conspired against me; there is none of you that is sorry for me" (1 Sam. xxii. 8.) Doeg is forward to curry favour by telling his tale, and so tells it as to suppress the priest's ignorance of David's flight, and to represent him as aiding and comforting the rebel knowingly. Then fierce wrath flames out from the darkened spirit, and the whole priestly population of Nob are summoned before him, loaded with bitter reproaches, their professions of innocence disregarded, and his guard ordered to murder them all then and there. The very soldiers shrink from the sacrilege, but a willing tool is at hand. The wild blood of Edom, fired by ancestral hatred, desires no better work, and Doeg crowns his baseness by slaying—with the help of his herdsmen, no doubt—" on that day fourscore and five persons that did wear an ephod," and utterly extirpating every living thing from the defenceless little city.

One psalm, the fifty-second, is referred by its inscription to this period, but the correspondence between the history and the tone of the psalm is doubtful. It is a vehement rebuke and a prophecy of destruction directed against an enemy, whose hostility was expressed in "devouring words." The portrait does not apply very accurately to the Doeg of the historical books, inasmuch as it describes the psalmist's enemy as " a mighty man,"—or rather as " a hero," and as trusting " in the abundance of his riches,"—

and makes the point of the reproach against him that he is a confirmed liar. But the dastardly deed of blood may be covertly alluded to in the bitterly sarcastic "hero"—as if he had said, "O brave warrior, who dost display thy prowess in murdering unarmed priests and women?" And Doeg's story to Saul was a lie in so far as it gave the impression of the priests' complicity with David, and thereby caused their deaths on a false charge. The other features of the description are not contrary to the narrative, and most of them are in obvious harmony with it. The psalm, then, may be taken as showing how deeply David's soul was stirred by the tragedy. He pours out broken words of hot and righteous indignation:

"Destructions doth thy tongue devise,
  Like a razor whetted—O thou worker of deceit."
  * * * * * *
"Thou lovest all words that devour :* O thou deceitful tongue!"

He prophesies the destruction of the cruel liar, and the exultation of the righteous when he falls, in words which do indeed belong to the old covenant of retribution, and yet convey an eternal truth which modern sentimentalism finds

* Literally, "words of swallowing up."

very shocking, but which is witnessed over and over again in the relief that fills the heart of nations and of individuals when evil men fade: "When the wicked perish, there is shouting"—

> "Also God shall smite thee down for ever,
> Will draw thee out,* and carry thee away from the tent,
> And root thee out of the land of the living;
> And the righteous shall see and fear,
> And over him shall they laugh."

In confident security he opposes his own happy fellowship with God to this dark tragedy of retribution:

> "But I—(I am) like a green olive tree in the house of God."

The enemy was to be "rooted out;" the psalmist is to flourish by derivation of life and vigour from God. If Robinson's conjecture that Nob was on the Mount of Olives were correct (which is very doubtful), the allusion here would gain appropriateness. As the olives grew all round the humble forest sanctuary, and were in some sort hallowed by the shrine which they encompassed, so the soul grows and is safe in loving fellowship with God. Be that

---

* The full force of the word is, "will pluck out as a glowing ember from a hearth" (Delitzsch).

as it may, the words express the outlaw's serene confidence that he is safe beneath the sheltering mercy of God, and re-echo the hopes of his earlier psalm, "I will dwell in the house of the Lord for ever." The stormy indignation of the earlier verses passes away into calm peace and patient waiting in praise and trust:

'I will praise Thee for ever, for Thou hast done (it),
And wait on Thy name in the presence of Thy beloved, for it is good."

Hunted from Nob, David with a small company struck across the country in a south-westerly direction, keeping to the safety of the tangled mountains, till, from the western side of the hills of Judah, he looked down upon the broad green plain of Philistia. Behind him was a mad tyrant, in front the uncircumcised enemies of his country and his God. His condition was desperate, and he had recourse to desperate measures. That nearest Philistine city, some ten miles off, on which he looked down from his height, was Gath; the glen where he had killed its champion was close beside him,— every foot of ground was familiar by many a foray and many a fight. It was a dangerous resource to trust himself in Gath, with Goliath's sword dangling in his belt. But he may have hoped that he was not known by person, or may have thought that Saul's famous commander would be a welcome guest, as a banished man, at the Philistine court. So he made the plunge, and took refuge in Goliath's city. Discovery soon came, and in the most ominous form. It was an ugly sign that the servants of Achish should be quoting the words of the chant of victory which extolled him as the slayer of their countryman. Vengeance for his death was but too likely to come next. The doubts of his identity seem to have lasted for some little time, and to have been at first privately communicated to the king. They somehow reached David, and awoke his watchful attention, as well as his fear. The depth of his alarm and his ready resource are shown by his degrading trick of assumed madness—certainly the least heroic action of his life. What a picture of a furious madman is the description of his conduct when Achish's servants came to arrest him. He "twisted himself about in their hands" in the feigned contortions of possession; he drummed on the leaves of the gate,* and "let his spittle run down into his beard." (1 Sam. xxi. 13.) Israelitish quickness gets the better of Philistine stupidity, as it had been used to do from Sampson's time onwards, and the dull-witted king falls into the trap, and laughs away the suspicions with a clumsy joke at his servants' expense about more madmen being the last thing he was short of. A hasty flight from Philistine territory ended this episode.

The fifty-sixth psalm, which is referred by its title to this period, seems at first sight to be in strange contrast with the impressions drawn from the narrative, but on a closer examination is found to confirm the correctness of the reference by its contents. The terrified fugitive, owing his safety to a trick, and slavering like an idiot in the hands of his rude captors, had an inner life of trust strong enough to hold his mortal terror in check, though not to annihilate it. The psalm is far in advance of the conduct—is it so unusual a circumstance as to occasion sur-

* The Septuagint appears to have followed a different reading here from that of our present Hebrew text, and the change adds a very picturesque clause to the description. A madman would be more likely to hammer than to "scrabble" on the great double-leaved gate.

prise, that lofty and sincere utterances of faith and submission should co-exist with the opposite feelings? Instead of taking the contrast between the words and the acts as a proof that this psalm is wrongly ascribed to the period in question, let us rather be thankful for another instance that imperfect faith may be genuine, and that if we cannot rise to the height of unwavering fortitude, God accepts a tremulous trust fighting against mortal terror, and grasping with a feeble hand the word of God, and the memory of all his past deliverances. It is precisely this conflict of faith and fear which the psalm sets before us. It falls into three portions, the first and second of which are closed by a kind of refrain (vers. 4, 10, 11)—a structure which is characteristic of several of these Sauline persecution psalms (*e.g.*, lvii. 5, 11; lix. 9, 17). The first part of each of these two portions is a vivid description of his danger, from which he rises to the faith expressed in the closing words. The repetition of the same thoughts in both is not to be regarded as a cold artifice of composition, but as the true expression of the current of his thoughts. He sees his enemies about him, ready to swallow him up—

"there be many fighting against me disdainfully"* (ver. 2). Whilst the terror creeps round his heart ("he was sore afraid," 1 Sam. xxi. 12), he rouses himself to trust, as he says, in words which express most emphatically the co-existence of the two, and carry a precious lesson of the reality of even an interrupted faith, streaked with many a black line of doubt and dread.

"(In) the day (that) I am afraid—I trust on Thee."

And then he breaks into the utterance of praise and confidence—to which he has climbed by the ladder of prayer.

> "In God I praise His word,
> In God I trust, I do not fear :—
> What shall flesh do to me?"

How profoundly these words set forth the object of his trust, as being not merely the promise of God—which in David's case may be the specific promise conveyed by his designation to the throne—but the God who promises, the inmost nature of that confidence as being a living union with God, the power of it as grapp-

---

* Literally, "loftily." Can there be any allusion to the giant stature of Goliath's relations in Gath? We hear of four men "born to the giant in Gath," who were killed in David's wars. (2 Sam. xxi. 22.)

ling with his dread, and enabling him now to say, "I do *not* fear."

But again he falls from this height; another surge of fear breaks over him, and almost washes him from his rock. His foes, with ceaseless malice, arrest his words; they skulk in ambush, they dog his heels, they long for his life. The crowded clauses portray the extremity of the peril and the singer's agitation. His soul is still heaving with the ground swell of the storm, though the blasts come more fitfully, and are dying into calm. He is not so afraid but that he can turn to God; he turns to Him because he is afraid, like the disciples in later days, who had so much of terror that they must awake their Master, but so much of trust that His awaking was enough. He pleads with God, as in former psalms, against his enemies, in words which go far beyond the occasion, and connect his own deliverance with the judgments of God over the whole earth. He plaintively recalls his homelessness and his sorrows in words which exhibit the characteristic blending of hope and pain, and which are beautifully in accordance with the date assigned to the psalm. "My wanderings dost Thou, even Thou, number."

He is not alone in these weary flights from Gibeah to Ramah, from Ramah to Nob, from Nob to Gath, from Gath he knows not whither. One friend goes with him through them all. And as the water-skin was a necessary part of a traveller's equipment, the mention of his wanderings suggests the bold and tender metaphor of the next clause, "Put my tears in Thy bottle," —a prayer for that very remembrance of his sorrows, in the existence of which he immediately declares his confidence—"Are they not in Thy book?" The true office of faithful communion with God is to ask for, and to appropriate, the blessings which in the very act become ours. He knows that his cry will scatter his foes, for God is for him. And thus once again he has risen to the height of confidence where for a moment his feet have been already planted, and again — but this time with even fuller emphasis, expressed by an amplification which introduces for the only time in the psalm the mighty covenant name—he breaks into his triumphant strain—

"In God I praise the Word;
In JEHOVAH I praise the Word;
In God I trust, I do not fear :—
What shall man do to me?"

And from this mood of trustful expectation he does not again decline. Prayer has brought its chiefest blessing—the peace that passeth understanding. The foe is lost to sight, the fear conquered conclusively by faith; the psalm which begins with a plaintive cry, ends in praise for deliverance, as if it had been already achieved—

"Thou hast delivered my life from death,
 (Hast Thou) not (delivered) my feet from falling,
 That I may walk before God in the light of the living?"

He already reckons himself safe; his question is not an expression of doubt, but of assurance; and he sees the purpose of all God's dealings with him to be that the activities of life may all be conducted in the happy consciousness of *His* eye who is at once Guardian and Judge of His children. How far above his fears and lies has this hero and saint risen by the power of supplication and the music of his psalm!

David naturally fled into Israelitish territory from Gath. The exact locality of the cave Adullam, where we next find him, is doubtful; but several strong reasons occur for rejecting the monkish tradition which places it away to the east, in one of the wild wadies which run down from Bethlehem to the Dead Sea. We should expect it to be much more accessible by a hasty march from Gath. Obviously it would be convenient for him to hang about the frontier of Philistia and Israel, that he might quickly cross the line from one to the other, as dangers appeared. Further, the city of Adullam is frequently mentioned, and always in connections which fix its site as on the margin of the great plain of Philistia, and not far from Gath. (2 Chron. xi. 7, etc.) There is no reason to suppose that the cave of Adullam was in a totally different district from the city. The hills of Dan and Judah, which break sharply down into the plain within a few miles of Gath, are full of "extensive excavations," and there, no doubt, we are to look for the rocky hold, where he felt himself safer from pursuit, and whence he could look down over the vast sweep of the rich Philistine country. Gath lay at his feet, close by was the valley where he had killed Goliath, the scenes of Samson's exploits were all about him. Thither fled to him his whole family, from fear, no doubt, of Saul's revenge falling on them; and there he gathers his band of four hundred desperate men, whom poverty and misery, and probably the king's growing tyranny, drove to flight. They were wild, rough soldiers, according to the picturesque description, "whose faces were like the faces of lions, and were as swift as the roes upon the mountains." They were not freebooters, but seem to have acted as a kind of frontier-guard against southern Bedouins and western Philistines for the sheep-farmers of the border whom Saul's government was too weak to protect. In this desultory warfare, and in eluding the pursuit of Saul, against whom it is to be observed David never employed any weapon but flight, several years were passed. The effect of such life on his spiritual nature was to deepen his unconditional dependence on God; by the alternations of heat and cold, fear and hope, danger and safety, to temper his soul and make it flexible, tough and bright as steel. It evolved the qualities of a leader of men; teaching him command and forbearance, promptitude and patience, valour and gentleness. It won for him a name as the defender of the nation, as Nabal's servant said of him and his men, "They were a wall unto us, both by night and by day" (1 Sam. xxv. 16). And it gathered round him a force of men devoted to him by the enthusiastic attachment bred from long years of common dangers, and the hearty friendships of many a march by day, and nightly encampment round the glimmering watchfires, beneath the lucid stars.

VI.—THE EXILE—*CONTINUED.*

WE have one psalm which the title connects with the beginning of David's stay at Adullam,—the thirty-fourth. The supposition that it dates from that period throws great force into many parts of it, and gives a unity to what is else apparently fragmentary and disconnected. Unlike those already considered, which were pure soliloquies, this is full of exhortation and counsel, as would naturally be the case if it were written when friends and followers began to gather to his standard. It reads like a long sigh of relief at escape from a danger just past; its burden is to tell of God's deliverance, and to urge to trust in Him. How perfectly this tone corresponds to the circumstances immediately after his escape from Gath to Adullam need not be more than pointed out. The dangers which he had dreaded and the cry to God which he had sent forth are still present to his mind, and echo through his song, like a subtly-touched chord of sadness, which appears for a moment, and is drowned in the waves of some triumphant music.

> " I sought the Lord, and He heard me,
>   And from all my alarms He delivered me.
>   *   *   *   *   *
>   This afflicted (man) cried, and Jehovah heard,
>   And from all his troubles He saved him."

And the "local colouring" of the psalm corresponds too with the circumstances of Adullam. How appropriate, for instance, does the form in which the Divine protection is proclaimed become, when we think of the little band bivouacking among the cliffs, "The angel of the Lord encampeth round about them that fear Him, and delivereth them." Like his great ancestor, he is met in his desert flight by heavenly guards, "and he calls the name of that place Mahanaim" (that is, "two camps"), as discerning gathered round his own feeble company the ethereal weapons of an encircling host of the warriors of God, through whose impenetrable ranks his foes must pierce before they can reach him. From Samson's time we read of lions in this district (Judges xiv. 8, 9), and we may recognise another image as suggested by their growls heard among the ravines, and their gaunt forms prowling near the cave. "The young lions do lack and suffer hunger; but they that seek the Lord shall not want any good" (ver. 10).

And then he passes to earnest instructions and exhortations, which derive appositeness from regarding them as a proclamation to his men of the principles on which his camp is to be governed. "Come, ye children, hearken unto me." He regards himself as charged with guiding them to godliness: "I will teach you the fear of the Lord." With some remembrance, perhaps, of his deception at Gath, he warns them to "keep" their "tongues from evil" and their "lips from speaking guile." They are not to be in love with warfare, but, even with their swords in their hands, are to "seek peace, and pursue it." On these exhortations follow joyous assurances of God's watchful eye fixed upon the righteous, and His ear open to their cry; of deliverance for his suppliants, whatsoever hardship and trouble they may have to wade through; of a guardianship which "keepeth all the bones" of the righteous, so that neither the blows of the foe nor the perils of the crags should break them, —all crowned with the contrast ever present to

David's mind, and having a personal reference to his enemies and to himself:

> "Evil shall slay the wicked,
> And the haters of the righteous shall suffer penalty.
> Jehovah redeems the life of His servants,
> And no penalty shall any suffer who trust in Him."

Such were the counsels and teachings of the young leader to his little band,—noble "general orders" from a commander at the beginning of a campaign!

We venture to refer the twenty-seventh psalm also to this period. It is generally supposed, indeed, by those commentators who admit its Davidic authorship, to belong to the time of Absalom's rebellion. The main reason for throwing it so late is the reference in ver. 4 to dwelling in the house of the Lord and inquiring in His temple.* This is supposed to require a date subsequent to David's bringing up of the ark to Jerusalem, and placing it in a temporary sanctuary. But whilst longing for the sanctuary is no doubt characteristic of the psalms of the

---

* "The fourth verse in its present form *must* have been written after the temple was built."—"The Psalms chronologically arranged," p. 68—following Ewald, in whose imperious criticism that same naked "must have been," works wonders.

later wanderings, it is by no means necessary to suppose that in the present case that desire, which David represents as the longing of his life, was a desire for mere bodily presence in a material temple. Indeed, the very language seems to forbid such an interpretation. Surely the desire for an abode in the house of the Lord —which was his one wish, which he longed to have continuous throughout all the days of his life, which was to surround him with a privacy of protection in trouble, and to be as the munitions of rocks about him—was something else than a morbid desire for an impossible seclusion in the tabernacle,—a desire fitter for some sickly mediæval monarch who buried his foolish head and faint heart in a monastery than for God's Anointed. We have seen an earlier germ of the same desire in the twenty-third psalm, the words of which are referred to here; and the interpretation of the one is the interpretation of the other. The psalmist breathes his longing for the Divine fellowship, which shall be at once vision, and guidance, and hidden life in distress, and stability, and victory, and shall break into music of perpetual praise.

If, then, we are not obliged by the words in

question to adopt the later date, there is much in the psalm which strikingly corresponds with the earlier, and throws beautiful illustration on the psalmist's mood at this period. One such allusion we venture to suppose in the words (ver. 2),

"When the wicked came against me to devour my flesh,
My enemies and my foes,—*they* stumbled and fell;"

which have been usually taken as a mere general expression, without any allusion to a specific event. But there was one incident in David's life which had been forced upon his remembrance by his recent peril at Gath—his duel with Goliath, which exactly meets the very peculiar language here. The psalm employs the same word as the narrative, which tells how the Philistine "arose, and came, and drew near to David." The braggart boast, "I will give thy flesh unto the fowls of the air and the beasts of the fields," is echoed in the singular phrase of the psalm; and the emphatic, rapid picture, "they stumbled and fell," is at once a reminiscence of the hour when the stone crashed through the thick forehead, "and he fell upon his face to the earth;" and also a reference to an earlier triumph in Israel's history, celebrated with fierce exultation in the wild chant which rolls the words like a sweet morsel under the tongue, as it tells of Sisera—

> "Between her feet he bowed, he fell, he lay ;
> Between her feet he bowed, he fell ;
> Where he bowed, there he fell down dead."

Another autobiographical reference in the psalm has been disputed on insufficient grounds :

> "For my father and my mother forsake me,
> And Jehovah takes me up." (Ver. 10.)

It is, at all events, a remarkable coincidence that the only mention of his parents after the earliest chapters of his life falls in precisely with this period of the history, and is such as might have suggested these words. We read (1 Sam. xxii. 3, 4) that he once ventured all the way from Adullam to Moab to beg an asylum from Saul's indiscriminate fury for his father and mother, who were no doubt too old to share his perils, as the rest of his family did. Having prepared a kindly welcome for them, perhaps on the strength of the blood of Ruth the Moabitess in Jesse's veins, he returned to Bethlehem, brought the old couple away, and guarded them safely to their refuge. It is surely most natural to suppose that the psalm is the lyrical echo of that event, and most pathetic to conceive of the psalmist as thinking of the happy home at Bethlehem now deserted, his brothers lurking with him among the rocks, and his parents exiles in heathen lands. Tears fill his eyes, but he lifts them to a Father that is never parted from him, and feels that he is no more orphaned nor homeless.

The psalm is remarkable for the abrupt transition of feeling which cleaves it into two parts; one (vers. 1—6) full of jubilant hope and enthusiastic faith, the other (vers. 7—14) a lowly cry for help. There is no need to suppose, with some critics, that we have here two independent hymns bound together in error. He must have little knowledge of the fluctuations of the devout life who is surprised to find so swift a passage from confidence to conscious weakness. Whilst the usual order in the psalms, as the usual order in good men's experience, is that prayer for deliverance precedes praise and triumph, true communion with God is bound to no mechanical order, and may begin with gazing on God, and realizing the mysteries of beauty in His secret place, ere it drops to earth.

The lark sings as it descends from the "privacy of glorious light" to its nest in the stony furrows as sweetly, though more plaintively, than whilst it circles upwards to the sky. It is perhaps a nobler effect of faith to begin with God and hymn the victory as if already won, than to begin with trouble and to call for deliverance. But with whichever we commence, the prayer of earth must include both; and so long as we are weak, and God our strength, its elements must be "supplication and thanksgiving." The prayer of our psalm bends round again to its beginning, and after the plaintive cry for help breaks once more into confidence (vers. 13, 14). The psalmist shudders as he thinks what ruin would have befallen him if he had not trusted in God, and leaves the unfinished sentence,—as a man looking down into some fearful gulf starts back and covers his eyes, before he has well seen the bottom of the abyss.

> "If I had not believed to see the goodness of the Lord in the land of the living!"

Then rejoicing to remember how even by his feeble trust he has been saved, he stirs up himself to a firmer faith, in words which are themselves an exercise of faith, as well as an incitement to it :

> "Wait on Jehovah !
> Courage ! and let thy heart be strong !
> Yea ! wait on Jehovah !"

Here is the true highest type of a troubled soul's fellowship with God, when the black fear and consciousness of weakness is inclosed in a golden ring of happy trust. Let the name of our God be first upon our lips, and the call to our wayward hearts to wait on Him be last, and then we may between think of our loneliness, and feebleness, and foes, and fears, without losing our hold of our Father's hand.

David in his rocky eyrie was joyful, because he began with God. It was a man in real peril who said, " The Lord is my light and my salvation, whom shall I fear ? " It was at a critical pause in his fortunes, when he knew not yet whether Saul's malice was implacable, that he said, " Though war should rise against me, in this will I be confident." It was in thankfulness for the safe hiding-place among the dark caverns of the hills that he celebrated the dwelling of the soul in God with words coloured by his circumstances, " In the secret of His tabernacle shall He hide me; He shall set me up upon a rock." It was with Philistia at his feet before and Saul's kingdom in arms behind that his triumphant confidence was sure that " Now shall mine head be lifted up above mine enemies round about me." It was in weakness, not expelled even by such joyous faith, that he plaintively besought God's mercy, and laid before His mercy-seat as the mightiest plea His own inviting words, " Seek ye My face," and His servant's humble response, " Thy face, Lord, will I seek." Together, these made it impossible that that Face, the beams of which are light and salvation, should be averted. God's past comes to his lips as a plea for a present consistent with it and with His own mighty name. "Thou hast been my help; leave me not, neither forsake me, O God of my salvation." His loneliness, his ignorance of his road, and the enemies who watch him, and, like a later Saul, " breathe out cruelty " (see Acts ix. 1), become to him in his believing petitions, not grounds of fear, but arguments with God; and having thus mastered all that was distressful in his lot, by making it all the basis of his cry for help, he rises again to hope, and stirs up himself to lay hold on God, to be strong and bold, because his expectation is from Him. A noble picture of a steadfast soul; steadfast not because of absence of fears and reasons for fear, but because of presence of God and faith in Him.

Having abandoned Adullam, by the advice of the prophet Gad, who from this time appears to have been a companion till the end of his reign (2 Sam. xxiv. 11), and who subsequently became his biographer (1 Chron. xxix. 29), he took refuge, as outlaws have ever been wont to do, in the woods. In his forest retreat, somewhere among the now treeless hills of Judah, he heard of a plundering raid made by the Philistines on one of the unhappy border towns. The marauders had broken in upon the mirth of the threshing-floors with the shout of battle, and swept away the year's harvest. The banished man resolved to strike a blow at the ancestral foes. Perhaps one reason may have been the wish to show that, outlaw as he was, he, and not the morbid laggard at Gibeah, who was only stirred to action by mad jealousy, was the sword of Israel. The little band bursts from the hills on the spoil-encumbered Philistines, recaptures the cattle which like moss-troopers they were driving homewards from the ruined farmsteads, and routs them with great slaughter. But the cowardly townspeople of Keilah had less gratitude than fear; and the king's banished son-in-law was too dangerous a guest, even though he was of their own tribe, and had delivered them from the enemy. Saul, who had not stirred from his moody seclusion to beat back invasion, summoned a hasty muster, in the hope of catching David in the little city, like a fox in his earth: and the cowardly citizens meditated saving their homes by surrendering their champion. David and his six hundred saved themselves by a rapid flight, and, as it would appear, by breaking up into detachments. "They went whithersoever they could go" (1 Sam. xxiii. 13); whilst David, with some handful, made his way to the inhospitable wilderness which stretches from the hills of Judah to the shores of the Dead Sea, and skulked there in "lurking places" among the crags and tangled underwood. With fierce perseverance "Saul sought him every day, but God delivered him not into his hand." One breath of love, fragrant and strength-giving, was wafted to his fainting heart, when Jonathan found his way where Saul could not come, and the two friends met once more. In the woodland solitudes they plighted their faith again, and the beautiful unselfishness of Jonathan is wonderfully set forth in his words, "Thou shalt be king over Israel, and I shall be next unto thee;" while an awful glimpse is given into that mystery of a godless will consciously resisting the inevitable, when there is added, "and that also Saul, my father, knoweth." In such resistance the king's son has no part, for it is pointedly noticed that he returned to his house. Treachery, and that from the men of his own tribe, again dogs David's steps. The people of Ziph, a small place on the edge of the southern desert, betray his haunt to Saul. The king receives the intelligence with a burst of thanks, in which furious jealousy and perverted religion, and a sense of utter loneliness and misery, and a strange self-pity, are mingled most pathetically and terribly: "Blessed be ye of the Lord, for ye have compassion on me!" He sends them away to mark down his prey; and when they have tracked him to his lair, he follows with his force and posts them round the hill where David and his handful lurk. The little band try to escape, but they are surrounded and apparently lost. At the very moment when the trap is just going to close, a sudden messenger, "fiery red with haste," rushes into Saul's army with news of a formidable invasion: "Haste thee and come; for the Philistines have spread themselves upon the land!" So the eager hand, ready to smite and crush, is plucked back; and the hour of deepest distress is the hour of deliverance.

At some period in this lowest ebb of David's fortunes, we have one short psalm, very simple and sad (liv.) It bears the title, "When the Ziphims came and said to Saul, Doth not David hide himself with us?" and may probably be referred to the former of the two betrayals by the men of Ziph. The very extremity of peril has made the psalmist still and quiet. The sore need has shortened his prayer. He is too sure that God hears to use many words; for it is distrust, not faith, which makes us besiege His throne with much speaking. He is confident as ever; but one feels that there is a certain self-restraint and air of depression over the brief petitions, which indicate the depth of his distress and the uneasiness of protracted anxiety. Two notes only sound from his harp: one a plaintive cry for help; the other, thanksgiving for deliverance as already achieved. The two are bound together by the recurrence in each of "the name" of GOD, which is at once the source of his salvation and the theme of his praise. We have only to read the lowly petitions to feel that they speak of a spirit somewhat weighed down by danger, and relaxed from the loftier mood of triumphant trust.

>(1) O God, by Thy name save me,
>   And in Thy strength do judgment for me.
>
>(2) O God, hear my prayer,
>   Give ear to the words of my mouth.
>
>(3) For strangers are risen against me,
>   And tyrants seek my life.
>   They set not God before them.

The enemies are called "strangers;" but, as we have seen in the first of these songs of the exile, it is not necessary, therefore, to suppose that they were not Israelites. The Ziphites were men of Judah like himself; and there is bitter emphasis as well as a gleam of insight into the spiritual character of the true Israel in calling them foreigners. The other name, oppressors, or violent men, or, as we have rendered it, tyrants, corresponds too accurately with the character of Saul in his later years, to leave much doubt that it is pointed at him. If so, the softening of the harsh description by the use of the plural is in beautiful accordance with the forgiving leniency which runs through all David's conduct to him. Hard words about Saul himself do not occur in the psalms. His counsellors, his spies, the liars who calumniated David to him, and for their own ends played upon his suspicious nature,—the tools who took care that the cruel designs suggested by themselves should be carried out, kindle David's wrath, but it scarcely ever lights on the unhappy monarch whom he loved with all-enduring charity while he lived, and mourned with magnificent eulogy when he died. The allusion is made all the more probable, because of the verbal correspondence with the narrative which records that "Saul was come out to seek his life" (1 Sam. xxiii. 15.)

A chord or two from the harp permits the mind to dwell on the thought of the foes, and prepares for the second part of this psalm. In it thanksgiving and confidence flow from the petitions of the former portion. But the praise is not so jubilant, nor the trust so victorious, as we have seen them. "The peace of God" has come in answer to prayer, but it is somewhat subdued:

> " Behold, God is my helper;
> The Lord is the supporter of my life."

The foes sought his life, but, as the historical book gives the antithesis, "Saul sought him every day, but God delivered him not into his hand." The rendering of the English version, "The Lord is with them that uphold my soul," is literally accurate, but does not convey the meaning of the Hebrew idiom. God is not regarded as one among many helpers, but as alone the supporter or upholder of his life. Believing that, the psalmist, of course, believes as a consequence that his enemies will be smitten with evil for their evil. The prophetic lip of faith calls things that are not as though they were. In the midst of his dangers he looks forward to songs of deliverance and glad sacrifices of praise; and the psalm closes with words that approach the more fervid utterances we have already heard, as if his song had raised his own spirit above its fears:

> (6) With willinghood will I sacrifice unto Thee.
> I will praise Thy name for it is good.

(7) For from all distress it has delivered me.
And on my enemies will mine eye see (my desire).

The name—the revealed character of God—was the storehouse of all the saving energies to which he appealed in verse 1. It is the theme of his praise when the deliverance shall have come. It is almost regarded here as equivalent to the Divine personality—it is good, *it* has delivered him. Thus, we may say that this brief psalm gives us as the single thought of a devout soul in trouble, the name of the Lord, and teaches by its simple pathos how the contemplation of God as He has made Himself known, should underlie every cry for help and crown every thanksgiving; whilst it may assure us that whosoever seeks for the salvation of that mighty name may, even in the midst of trouble, rejoice as in an accomplished deliverance. And all such thoughts should be held with a faith at least as firm as the ancient psalmist's, by us to whom the "name" of the Lord is "declared" by Him who is the full revelation of God, and the storehouse of all blessings and help to his "brethren." (Heb. ii. 12.)

A little plain of some mile or so in breadth slopes gently down towards the Dead Sea about the centre of its western shore. It is girdled round by savage cliffs, which, on the northern side, jut out in a bold headland to the water's edge. At either extremity is a stream flowing down a deep glen choked with luxurious vegetation; great fig-trees, canes, and maiden-hair ferns covering the rocks. High up on the hills forming its western boundary a fountain sparkles into light, and falls to the flat below in long slender threads. Some grey weathered stones mark the site of a city that was old when Abraham wandered in the land. Traces of the palm forests which, as its name indicates, were cleared for its site (Hazezon Tamar, The palm-tree clearing) have been found, encrusted with limestone, in the warm, damp gullies, and ruined terraces for vineyards can be traced on the bare hill-sides. But the fertility of David's time is gone, and the precious streams nourish only a jungle haunted by leopard and ibex. This is the fountain and plain of Engedi (the fount of the wild goat), a spot which wants but industry and care to make it a little paradise. Here David fled from the neighbouring wilderness, attracted no doubt by the safety of the deep gorges and rugged hills, as well as by the abundance of water in the fountain and the streams. The picturesque and touching episode of his meeting with Saul has made the place for ever memorable. There are many excavations in the rocks about the fountain, which may have been the cave—black as night to one looking inward with eyes fresh from the blinding glare of sunlight upon limestone, but holding a glimmering twilight to one looking outwards with eyes accustomed to the gloom—in the innermost recesses of which David lay hid while Saul tarried in its mouth. The narrative gives a graphic picture of the hurried colloquy among the little band, when summary revenge was thus unexpectedly put within their grasp. The fierce retainers whispered their suggestion that it would be "tempting providence" to let such an opportunity escape; but the nobler nature of David knows no personal animosity, and in these earliest days is flecked by no cruelty nor lust of blood. He cannot, however, resist the temptation of showing his power and almost parading his forbearance by stealing through the darkness and cutting away the end of Saul's long robe. It was little compared with what he could as easily have done—smite him to the heart as he crouched there defenceless. But it was a coarse practical jest, conveying a rude insult, and the quickly returning nobleness of his nature made him ashamed of it, as soon as he had clambered back with his trophy. He felt that the sanctity of Saul's office as the anointed of the Lord should have saved him from the gibe. The king goes his way all unawares, and, as it would seem, had not regained his men, when David, leaving his band (very much out of temper no doubt at his foolish nicety), yields to a gush of ancient friendship and calls loudly after him, risking discovery and capture in his generous emotion. The pathetic conversation which ensued is eminently characteristic of both men, so tragically connected and born to work woe to one another. David's remonstrance (1 Sam. xxiv. 9—15) is full of nobleness, of wounded affection surviving still, of conscious rectitude, of solemn devout appeal to the judgment of God. He has no words of reproach for Saul, no weak upbraidings, no sullen anger, no repaying hate with hate. He almost pleads with the unhappy king, and yet there is nothing undignified or feeble in his tone. The whole is full of correspondences, often of verbal identity, with the psalms which we assign to this period. The calumnies which he so often complains of in these are the subject of his first words to Saul, whom he regards as having had his heart poisoned by lies: "Wherefore hearest thou men's words, saying, Behold! David seeketh thy hurt." He asserts absolute innocence of anything that warranted the king's hostility, just as he does so decisively in the psalms. "There is neither evil nor transgression in my hand, and I have not sinned against thee." As in them he so often compares himself to some wild creature pursued like the goats in the cliffs of Engedi, so he tells Saul, "Thou huntest my life to take it." And his appeal from earth's slanders, and misconceptions, and cruelties, to the perfect tribunal of God, is couched in language, every clause of which may be found in his psalms. "The Lord, therefore, be judge, and judge between me and thee, and see, and plead my cause, and deliver me out of thy hand."

The unhappy Saul again breaks into a passion of tears. With that sudden flashing out into vehement emotion so characteristic of him, and so significant of his enfeebled self-control, he recognises David's generous forbearance and its contrast to his own conduct. For a moment, at all events, he sees, as by a lightning flash, the mad hopelessness of the black road he is treading in resisting the decree that has made his rival king—and he binds him by an oath to spare his house when he sits on the throne. The picture moves awful thoughts and gentle pity for the poor scathed soul writhing in its hopelessness and dwelling in a great solitude of fear, but out of which stray gleams of ancient nobleness still break;—and so the doomed man goes back to his gloomy seclusion at Gibeah, and David to the free life of the mountains and the wilderness.

VII.—THE EXILE—*CONTINUED.*

THERE are many echoes of this period of Engedi in the Psalms. Perhaps the most distinctly audible of these are to be found in the seventh psalm, which is all but universally recognised as David's, even Ewald concurring in the general consent. It is an irregular ode—for such is the meaning of Shiggaion in the title, and by its broken rhythms and abrupt transitions testifies to the emotion of its author. The occasion of it is said to be "the words of Cush the Benjamite." As this is a peculiar name for an Israelite, it has been supposed to be an allegorical designation for some historical person, expressive of his character. We might render it "the negro." The Jewish commentators have taken it to refer to Saul himself, but the bitter tone of the psalm, so unlike David's lingering forbearance to the man whom he never ceased to love, is against that supposition. Shimei the Benjamite, whose foul tongue cursed him in rabid rage, as he fled before Absalom, has also been thought of, but the points of correspondence with the earlier date are too numerous to make that reference tenable. It seems better to suppose that Cush "the black" was one of Saul's tribe, who had been conspicuous among the calumniators of whom we have seen David complaining to the king. And if so, there is no period in the Sauline persecution into which the psalm will fit so naturally as the present. Its main thoughts are precisely those which he poured out so passionately in his eager appeal when he and Saul stood face to face on the solitary hill side. They are couched in the higher strain of poetry indeed, but that is the only difference; whilst there are several verbal coincidences, and at least one reference to the story, which seem to fix the date with considerable certainty.

In it we see the psalmist's soul surging with the ground swell of strong emotion, which breaks into successive waves of varied feeling—first (vers. 1, 2) terror blended with trust, the enemy pictured, as so frequently in these early psalms, as a lion who tears the flesh and breaks the bones of his prey—and the refuge in God described by a graphic word very frequent also in the cotemporaneous psalms (xi. 1 ; lvii. 1, etc.). Then with a quick turn comes the passionate protestation of his innocence, in hurried words, broken by feeling, and indignantly turning away from the slanders which he will not speak of more definitely than calling them "this."

(3) Jehovah, my God ! if I have done this—
    If there be iniquity in my hands—

(4) If I have rewarded evil to him that was at peace with me—
    Yea, I delivered him that without cause is mine enemy—

(5) May the enemy pursue my soul and capture it,
    And trample down to the earth my life,
    And my glory in the dust may he lay !

How remarkably all this agrees with his words to Saul, "There is neither evil nor transgression in my hand, ... yet thou huntest my soul to take it" (1 Sam. xxiv. 11); and how forcible becomes the singular reiteration in the narrative, of the phrase "my hand," which occurs six times in four verses. The peculiarly abrupt introduction in ver. 4 of the clause, "I delivered him that without cause is mine enemy," which completely dislocates the grammatical structure, is best accounted for by supposing that David's mind is still full of the temptation to stain his hands with Saul's blood, and is vividly conscious of the effort which he had had to make to overcome it. And the solemn invocation of destruction which he dares to address to Jehovah his God includes the familiar figure of himself as a fugitive before the hunters, which is found in the words already quoted, and which here as there stands in immediate connection with his assertion of clean hands.

Then follows, with another abrupt turn, a vehement cry to God to judge his cause; his own individual case melts into the thought of a world-wide judgment, which is painted with grand power with three or four broad rapid strokes.

(6) Awake for me—Thou hast commanded judgment.
(7) Let the assembly of the nations stand round Thee,
    And above it return Thou up on high.
(8) Jehovah will judge the nations.
    Judge me, O Jehovah, according to my righteousness
    and mine integrity in me!

Each smaller act of God's judgment is connected with the final world-judgment, is a prophecy of it, is one in principle therewith; and He, who at the last will be known as the universal Judge of all, certainly cannot leave His servants' cause unredressed nor their cry unheard till then. The psalmist is led by his own history to realize more intensely that truth of a Divine manifestation for judicial purposes to the whole world, and his prophetic lip paints its solemnities as the surest pledge of his own deliverance. He sees the gathered nations standing hushed before the Judge, and the Victor God at the close of the solemn act ascending up on high where He was before, above the heads of the mighty crowd (Psalm lxviii. 19). In the faith of this vision, and because God will judge the nations, he invokes for himself the anticipation of that final triumph of good over evil, and asks to be dealt with according to his righteousness. Nothing but the most hopeless determination to find difficulties could make a difficulty of such words. David is not speaking of his whole character or life, but of his conduct in one specific matter, namely, in his relation to Saul. The righteous integrity which he calls God to vindicate is not general sinlessness nor inward conformity with the law of God, but his blamelessness in all his conduct to his gratuitous foe. His prayer that God would judge him is distinctly equivalent to his often repeated cry for deliverance, which should, as by a Divine arbitration, decide the debate between Saul and him. The whole passage in the psalm, with all its lyrical abruptness and lofty imagery, is the expression of the very same thought which we find so prominent in his words to Saul, already quoted, concerning God's judging between them and delivering David out of Saul's hand. The parallel is instructive, not only as the prose rendering of the poetry in the psalm, explaining it beyond the possibility of misunderstanding, but also as strongly confirmatory of the date which we have assigned to the latter. It is so improbable as to be almost inconceivable that the abrupt disconnected themes of the psalm should echo so precisely the *whole* of the arguments used in the remonstrance of the historical books, and should besides present verbal resemblances and historical allusions to these, unless it be of the same period, and therefore an inlet into the mind of the fugitive as he lurked among the rugged cliffs by " the fountain of the wild goat."

In that aspect the remainder of the psalm is

very striking and significant. We have two main thoughts in it—that of God as punishing evil in this life, and that of the self-destruction inherent in all sin; and these are expressed with such extraordinary energy as to attest at once the profound emotion of the psalmist, and his familiarity with such ideas during his days of persecution. It is noticeable, too, that the language is carefully divested of all personal reference; he has risen to the contemplation of a great law of the Divine government, and at that elevation the enemies whose calumnies and cruelties had driven him to God fade into insignificance.

With what magnificent boldness he paints God the Judge arraying Himself in His armour of destruction!

    (11 God is a righteous Judge,
         And a God (who is) angry every day.
    (12) If he (*i.e.*, the evil-doer) turn not, He whets His sword,
         His bow He has bent, and made it ready.
    (13) And for him He has prepared weapons of death,
         His arrows He has made blazing darts.

Surely there is nothing grander in any poetry than this tremendous image, smitten out with so few strokes of the chisel, and as true as it is grand. The representation applies to the facts of life, of which as directed by a present Providence, and not of any future retribution, David is here thinking. Among these facts is chastisement falling upon obstinate antagonism to God. Modern ways of thinking shrink from such representations; but the whole history of the world teems with confirmation of their truth— only what David calls the flaming arrows of God, men call "the natural consequences of evil." The later revelation of God in Christ brings into greater prominence the disciplinary character of all punishment here, but bates no jot of the intensity with which the earlier revelation grasped the truth of God as a righteous Judge in eternal opposition to, and aversion from, evil.

With that solemn picture flaming before his inward eye, the prophet-psalmist turns to gaze on the evil-doer who has to bear the brunt of these weapons of light. Summoning us to look with him by a "Behold!" he tells his fate in an image of frequent occurrence in the psalms of this period, and very natural in the lips of a man wandering in the desert among wild creatures, and stumbling sometimes into the traps dug for them: "He has dug a hole and hollowed it out, and he falls into the pitfall he is making." The crumbling soil in which he digs makes his footing on the edge more precarious with every spadeful that he throws out, and at last, while he is hard at work, in he tumbles. It is the conviction spoken in the proverbs of all nations, expressed here by David in a figure drawn from life—the conviction that all sin digs its own grave and is self-destructive. The psalm does not proclaim the yet deeper truth that this automatic action, by which sin sets in motion its own punishment, has a disciplinary purpose, so that the arrows of God wound for healing, and His armour is really girded on for, even while it seems to be against, the sufferer. But it would not be difficult to show that that truth underlies the whole Old Testament doctrine of retribution, and is obvious in many of David's psalms. In the present one the deliverance of the hunted prey is contemplated as the end of the baffled trapper's fall into his own snare, and beyond that the psalmist's thoughts do not travel. His own safety, the certainty that his appeal to God's judgment will not be in vain, fill his mind; and without following the fate of his enemy further, he closes this song of tumultuous and varied emotion with calm confidence and a vow of thanksgiving for a deliverance which is already as good as accomplished:

> (17) I will give thanks to Jehovah according to His righteousness,
> And I will sing the name of Jehovah, Most High.

We have still another psalm (lvii.) which is perhaps best referred to this period. According to the title, it belongs to the time when David "fled from Saul in the cave." This may, of course, apply to either Adullam or Engedi, and there is nothing decisive to be alleged for either; yet one or two resemblances to psalm vii. incline the balance to the latter period.

These resemblances are the designation of his enemies as lions (vii. 2; lvii. 4); the image of their falling into their own trap (vii. 15; lvii. 6); the use of the phrase "my honour" or "glory" for "my soul" (vii. 5; lvii. 8—the same word in the original); the name of God as "Most High" (vii. 17; lvii. 2), an expression which only occurs twice besides in the Davidic psalms (ix. 2; xxi. 7); the parallelism in sense between the petition which forms the centre and the close of the one, "Be Thou exalted, O God, above the heavens" (lvii. 5, 11), and that which is the most emphatic desire of the other, "Arise, O Lord, awake, . . . lift up Thyself for me" (vii. 6). Another correspondence, not preserved in our English version, is the employment in both of a rare poetical word, which originally means "to complete," and so comes naturally to have the secondary significations of "to perfect" and "to put an end to." The word in question only occurs five times in the Old Testament, and always in psalms. Four of these are in hymns ascribed to David, of which two are (lvii. 2), "The God that *performeth* all things for me," and (vii. 9), "Let the wickedness of the wicked *come to an end*." The use of the same peculiar word in two such dissimilar connections seems to show that it was, as we say, "running in his head" at the time, and is, perhaps, a stronger presumption of the cotemporaneousness of both psalms than its employment in both with the same application would have been.

Characteristic of these early psalms is the occurrence of a refrain (compare lvi. and lix.) which in the present instance closes both of the portions of which the hymn consists. The former of these (1—5) breathes prayerful trust, from which it passes to describe the encompassing dangers; the second reverses this order, and beginning with the dangers and distress, rises to ringing gladness and triumph, as though the victory were already won. The psalmist's confident cleaving of soul to God is expressed (ver. 1) by an image that may be connected with his circumstances at Engedi: "In Thee has my soul taken refuge." The English version is correct as regards the sense, though it obliterates the beautiful metaphor by its rendering "trusteth." The literal meaning of the verb is "to flee to a refuge," and its employment here may be due to the poetical play of the imagination, which likens his secure retreat among the everlasting hills to the safe hiding-place which his spirit found in God his habitation. A similar analogy appears in the earliest use of the expression, which may have been floating in the psalmist's memory, and which occurs in the ancient song of Moses (Deut. xxxii.). The scenery of the forty years' wanderings remarkably colours that ode, and explains the frequent recurrence in it of the name of God as "the

Rock." We have false gods, too, spoken of in it, as, "Their rock in whom they took refuge," where the metaphor appears in its completeness (ver. 37). Our psalm goes on with words which contain a further allusion to another part of the same venerable hymn, "And in the shadow of Thy wings will I take refuge," which remind us of the grand image in it of God's care over Israel, as of the eagle bearing her eaglets on her mighty pinions (ver. 11), and point onwards to the still more wonderful saying in which all that was terrible and stern in the older figure is softened into tenderness, and instead of the fierce affection of the mother eagle, the hen gathering her chickens under her wings becomes the type of the brooding love and more than maternal solicitude of God in Christ. Nor can we forget that the only other instance of the figure before David's psalms is in the exquisite idyl which tells of the sweet heroism of David's ancestress, Ruth, on whose gentle and homeless head was pronounced the benediction, "A full reward be given thee of the Lord God of Israel, under whose wings thou art come to trust" Ruth ii. 12). We may perhaps also see in this clause an extension of the simile which unquestionably lies in the verb, and may think of the strong "sides of the cave," arching above the fugitive like a gigantic pair of wings beneath which he nestles warm and dry, while the short-lived storm roars among the rocks—a type of that broad pinion which is his true defence till threatening evils be overpast. In the past he has sheltered his soul in God, but no past act of faith can avail for present distresses. It must be perpetually renewed. The past deliverances should make the present confidence more easy; and the true use of all earlier exercises of trust is to prepare for the resolve that we will still rely on the help we have so often proved. "I have trusted in Thee" should ever be followed by "And in the shadow of Thy wings will I trust."

The psalmist goes on to fulfil his resolve. He takes refuge by prayer in God, whose absolute elevation above all creatures and circumstances is the ground of his hope, whose faithful might will accomplish its design, and complete His servant's lot. "I will call to God Most High; to God who perfects (His purpose) for me." And then assured hope gleams upon his soul, and though the storm-clouds hang low and black as ever, they are touched with light. "He will send from heaven and save me." But even while this happy certainty dawns upon him, the contending fears, which ever lurk hard by faith, reassert their power, and burst in, breaking the flow of the sentence, which by its harsh construction indicates the sudden irruption of disturbing thoughts. "He that would swallow me up reproaches (me)." With this two-worded cry of pain—prolonged by the very unusual occurrence, in the middle of a verse, of the "Selah," which is probably a musical direction for the accompaniment—a billow of terror breaks over his soul; but its force is soon spent, and the hope, above which for a moment it had rolled, rises from the broken spray like some pillared light round which the surges dash in vain. "God shall send forth His mercy and His truth"—those two white-robed messengers who draw nigh to all who call on Him. Then follows in broken words, the true rendering of which is matter of considerable doubt, a renewed picture of his danger:

> (4) (With) my soul—among lions will I lie down.
> Devourers are the sons of men;
> Their teeth a spear and arrows,
> And their tongue a sharp sword.

The psalmist seems to have broken off the construction, and instead of finishing the sentence as he began it, to have substituted the first person for the third, which ought to have followed "my soul." This fragmentary construction expresses agitation of spirit. It may be a question whether the "lions" in the first clause are to be regarded as a description of his enemies, who are next spoken of without metaphor as sons of men who devour (or who "breathe out fire"), and whose words are cutting and wounding as spear and sword. The analogy of the other psalms of this period favours such an understanding of the words. But, on the other hand, the reference preferred by Delitzsch and others gives great beauty. According to that interpretation, the fugitive among the savage cliffs prepares himself for his nightly slumbers in calm confidence, and lays himself down there in the cave, while the wild beasts, whose haunt it may have been, prowl without, feeling himself safer among them than among the more ferocious "sons of men," whose hatred has a sharper tooth than even theirs. And then this portion of the psalm closes with the refrain, "Be Thou exalted, O God, above the heavens:

let Thy glory be above all the earth." A prayer that God would show forth His power, and exalt His name by delivering His servant. What lofty conviction that his cause was God's cause, that the Divine honour was concerned in his safety, that he was a chosen instrument to make known God's praise over all the world! —and what self-forgetfulness in that, even whilst he prays for his own deliverance, he thinks of it rather as the magnifying of God, than as it affects himself personally!

The second part continues the closing strain of the former, and describes the plots of his foes in the familiar metaphor of the pit, into which they fall themselves. The contemplation of this divine Nemesis on evil-doers leads up to the grand burst of thanksgiving with which the psalm closes—

(7) Fixed is my heart, O God! fixed my heart!
I will sing and strike the harp.*

(8) Awake, my glory! awake psaltery and harp!†
I will awake the dawn.

If the former part may be regarded as the

* Properly, "sing with a musical accompaniment."
† Two kinds of stringed instrument, the difference between which is very obscure.

evening song of confidence, this is the morning hymn of thankfulness. He lay down in peace among lions; he awakes to praise. He calls upon his soul to shake off slumber; he invokes the chords of his harp to arouse from its chamber the sleeping dawn. Like a mightier than himself, he will rise a great while before day, and the clear notes of the rude lyre, his companion in all his wanderings, will summon the morning to add its silent speech to His praise. But a still loftier thought inspires him. This hunted solitary not only knows that his deliverance is certain, but he has already the consciousness of a world-wide vocation, and anticipates that the story of his sorrow and his trust, with the music of his psalms, belong to the world, and will flow over the barriers of his own generation and of his own land into the whole earth—

(9) I will praise Thee among the peoples, O Lord,
I will strike the harp to Thee among the nations.

(10) For great unto the heavens is Thy mercy,
And to the clouds Thy truth.

These two mighty messengers of God, whose coming he was sure of (ver. 3), will show themselves in his deliverance, boundless and filling all the creation. They shall be the theme of his world-wide praise. And then with the repetition of the refrain the psalm comes round again to supplication, and dies into silent waiting before God till He shall be pleased to answer. Thus triumphant were the hopes of the lonely fugitive skulking in the wilderness; such bright visions peopled the waste places, and made the desert to rejoice and blossom as the rose.

The cxlii. is also, according to the title, one of the cave-psalms. But considerable doubt attaches to the whole group of so-called Davidic compositions in the last book of the psalter (p. 138—144), from their place, and from the fact that there are just seven of them, as well as in some cases from their style and character. They are more probably later hymns in David's manner. The one in question corresponds in tone with the psalms which we have been considering. It breathes the same profound consciousness of desolation and loneliness: "My spirit is darkened within me;" "Refuge fails me, no man cares for my soul." It glows with the same ardour of personal trust in and love to God which spring from his very loneliness and helplessness: "I cry unto Thee, O Jehovah! I say Thou art my refuge and my portion in the land of the living." It triumphs with the same confidence, and with the same conviction that his deliverance concerns all the righteous: "They shall *crown themselves in me*, for Thou hast dealt bountifully with me;" for such would appear to be the true meaning of the word rendered in our version "compass me about;" the idea being that the mercy of God to the psalmist would become a source of festal gladness to all His servants, who would bind the story of God's bounty to him upon their brows like a coronal for a banquet.

VIII.—THE EXILE—*CONTINUED.*

AS our purpose in this volume is not a complete biography, it will not be necessary to dwell on the subsequent portions of the exile, inasmuch as there is little reference to these in the psalms. We must pass over even that exquisite episode of Abigail, whose graceful presence and "most subtle flow of silver-paced counsel" soothed David's ruffled spirit, and led him captive at once as in a silken leash. The glimpse of old-world ways in the story, the rough mirth of the shearers, the hint of the kind of black mail by which David's little force was provided, the snarling humour and garrulous crustiness of Nabal, David's fierce blaze of hot wrath, the tribute of the shepherds to the kindliness and honour of the outlaws, the rustic procession, with the gracious lady last of all, the stately courtesy of the meeting, her calm wise words—not flattery, yet full of predictions of prosperity most pleasant to hear from such lips;

not rebuke, yet setting in the strongest light how unworthy of God's anointed personal vengeance was; not servile, but yet recognising in delicate touches his absolute power over her; not abject, and yet full of supplication,—the quick response of David's frank nature and susceptible heart, which sweeps away all his wrath; the budding germ of love, which makes him break into benedictions on her and her wisdom, and thankfulness that he had been kept back from "hurting *thee*," and the dramatic close in their happy union,—all make up one of the most charming of the many wonderful idyls of Scripture, all fragrant with the breath of love, and fresh with undying youth. The story lives —alas! how much longer do words endure than the poor earthly affections which they record!

After a second betrayal by the men of Ziph, and a second meeting with Saul—their last— in which the doomed man parts from him with blessing and predictions of victory on his unwilling lips, David seems to have been driven to desperation by his endless skulking in dens and caves, and to have seen no hope of continuing much longer to maintain himself on the frontier and to elude Saul's vigilance. Possibly others than Nabal grudged to pay him for the volunteer police which he kept up on behalf of the pastoral districts exposed to the wild desert tribes. At all events he once more made a plunge into Philistine territory, and offers himself and his men to the service of the King of Gath. On the offer being accepted, the little town of Ziklag was allotted to them, and became their home for a year and four months.

To this period of comparative security one psalm has been supposed to belong—the xxxi., which, in tone and in certain expressions, corresponds very well with the circumstances. There are many similarities in it with the others of the same period which we have already considered —such, for instance, as the figure of God his rock (ver. 3), the net which his enemies have laid for him (ver. 4), the allusions to their calumnies and slanders (vers. 13, 18), his safe concealment in God (ver. 20 : compare xxvii. 5 ; lvii. 1 ; xvii. 8, etc.), and the close verbal resemblance of ver. 24 with the closing words of psalm xxvii. The reference, however, which has been taken as pointing to David's position in Ziklag is that contained in the somewhat remarkable words (ver. 21) : "Blessed be the Lord, for He hath showed me His marvellous loving-kindness in a strong city." Of course, the expression may be purely a graphic figure for the walls and defences of the Divine protection, as, indeed, it is usually understood to be. But the general idea of the encompassing shelter of God has just been set forth in the magnificent imagery of the previous verse as the tabernacle, the secret of His presence in which He hides and guards His servants. And the further language of the phrase in question, introduced as it is by a rapturous burst of blessing and praise, seems so emphatic and peculiar as to make not unnatural the supposition of a historical basis in some event which had recently happened to the psalmist.

No period of the life will so well correspond to such a requirement as the sixteen months of his stay in Ziklag, during which he was completely free from fear of Saul, and stood high in favour with the King of Gath, in whose territory he had found a refuge. We may well believe that to the hunted exile, so long accustomed to a life of constant alarms and hurried flight, the quiet of a settled home was very sweet, and that behind the rude fortifications of the little town in the southern wilderness there seemed security, which made a wonderful contrast to their defenceless lairs and lurking-places among the rocks. Their eyes would lose their watchful restlessness, and it would be possible to lay aside their weapons, to gather their households about them, and, though they were in a foreign land, still to feel something of the bliss of peaceful habitudes and tranquil use and wont healing their broken lives. No wonder, then, that such thankful praise should break from the leader's lips! No wonder that he should regard this abode in a fortified city as the result of a miracle of Divine mercy! He describes the tremulous despondency which had preceded this marvel of loving-kindness in language which at once recalls the wave of hopelessness which swept across his soul after his final interview with Saul, and which led to his flight into Philistine territory, "And David said in his heart, I shall now perish one day by the hand of Saul" (1 Sam. xxvii. 1). How completely this corresponds with the psalm, allowance being made for the difference between poetry and prose, when he describes the thoughts which had shaded his soul just before the happy peace of the strong city—"I said in my haste,* I am cut off from before Thine eyes; nevertheless Thou heardest the voice of my supplication" (ver. 22). And rising, as was ever his manner, from his own individual experience to the great truths concerning God's care of His children, the discovery of which was to him even more precious than his personal safety, he breaks forth in jubilant invocation, which, as always, is full of his consciousness that his life and his story belong to the whole household of God—

> (23) O love Jehovah, all ye beloved of Him!
> The faithful doth Jehovah preserve,
> And plentifully repayeth the proud-doer.
>
> (24) Courage! and let your heart be strong,
> All ye that wait for Jehovah!

The glow of personal attachment to Jehovah which kindles in the trustful words is eminently characteristic. It anticipates the final teaching of the New Testament in bringing all the relations between God and the devout soul down to the one bond of love. "We love Him because He first loved us," says John. And David has

---

* Confusion (Perowne), distrust (Delitzsch), anguish (Ewald), trepidation (Calvin). The word literally means to sway backwards and forwards, and hence to be agitated by any emotion, principally by fear; and then, perhaps, to flee in terror.

the same discernment that the basis of all must be the outgoing of love from the heart of God, and that the only response which that seeking love requires is the awaking of the echo of its own Divine voice in our hearts. Love begets love; love seeks love; love rests in love. Our faith *corresponds* to His faithfulness, our obedience to His command, our reverence to His majesty; but our love *resembles* His, from which it draws its life. So the one exhortation is "love the Lord," and the ground of it lies in that name—"His beloved"—those to whom He shows His loving-kindness (ver. 21).

The closing words remind us of the last verse of psalm xxvii. They are distinctly quoted from it, with the variation that there the heartening to courage was addressed to his own soul, and here to "all who wait on the Lord." The resemblance confirms the reference of both psalms to the same epoch, while the difference suits the change in his circumstances from a period of comparative danger, such as his stay at Adullam, to one of greater security, like his residence in Ziklag. The same persons who were called to love the Lord because they were participant of His loving-kindness, are now called to courage and manly firmness of soul because their hope is fixed on Jehovah. The progress of thought is significant and obvious. Love to God, resting on consciousness of His love to us, is the true armour. "There is no fear in love." The heart filled with it is strong to resist the pressure of outward disasters, while the empty heart is crushed like a deserted hulk by the grinding collision of the icebergs that drift rudderless on the wild wintry sea of life. Love, too, is the condition of hope. The patience and expectation of the latter must come from the present fruition of the sweetness of the former. Of these fair sisters, Love is the elder as the greater; it is she who bears in her hands the rich metal from which Hope forges her anchor, and the strong cords that hold it; her experience supplies all the colours with which her sister paints the dim distance; and she it is who makes the other bold to be sure of the future, and clear-sighted to see the things that are not as though they were. To love the Lord is the path, and the only path, to hoping in the Lord. So had the psalmist found it for himself. In his changeful, perilous years of exile he had learned that the brightness with which hope glowed on his lonely path depended not on the accident of greater or less external security, but on the energy of the clear flame of love in his heart. Not in vain had his trials been to him, which cast that rich treasure to his feet from their stormy waves. Not in vain will ours be to us, if we learn the lesson which he here would divide with all those "that wait on the Lord."

Our limits prevent the further examination of the remaining psalms of this period. It is the less necessary, inasmuch as those which have been already considered fairly represent the whole. The xi., xiii., xvii., xxii., xxv., and lxiv. may, with varying probability, be considered as belonging to the Sauline persecution. To this list some critics would add the xl. and lxix., but on very uncertain grounds. But if we exclude them, the others have a strong family likeness, not only with each other, but with those which have been presented to the reader. The imagery of the wilderness, which has become so familiar to us, continually reappears; the prowling wild beasts, the nets and snares, the hunted psalmist like a timid bird among the hills; the protestation of innocence, the passionate invocation of retribution on the wicked, the confidence that their own devices will come down on their heads, the intense yearning of soul after God—are all repeated in these psalms. Single metaphors and peculiar phrases which we have already met with recur—as, for instance, "the shadow of Thy wings" (xvii. 8, lvii. 1), and the singular phrase rendered in our version, "show Thy marvellous loving-kindness" (xvii. 7, xxxi. 21), which is found only here. In one of these psalms (xxxv. 13) there seems to be a reference to his earliest days at the court, and to the depth of loving sympathy with Saul's darkened spirit, which he learned to cherish, as he stood before him to soothe him with the ordered harmonies of harp and voice. The words are so definite that they appear to refer to some historic occasion :

> And as for me—in their sickness my clothing was sackcloth,
> With fasting I humbled my soul,
> And my prayer into my own bosom returned.

So truly did he feel for him who is now his foe. The outward marks of mourning became the natural expression of his feelings. Such is plainly the meaning of the two former clauses, as well as of the following verse. As the whole is a description of the outward signs of grief, it seems better to understand the last of these three clauses as a picture of the bent head, sunk on the bosom even while he prayed,* than to break the connection by referring it either to the requital of hate for his sympathy,† or to the purity of his prayer, which was such that he could desire nothing more for himself.‡ He goes on with the enumeration of the signs of sorrow: "As if (he had been) a friend, a brother to me, I went,"—walking slowly, like a man absorbed in sorrow: "as one who laments a mother, in mourning garments I bowed down," —walking with a weary, heavy stoop, like one crushed by a mother's death, with the garb of woe. Thus faithfully had he loved, and truly wept for the noble ruined soul which, blinded by passion and poisoned by lies, had turned to be his enemy. And that same love clung by him to the last, as it ever does with great and good men, who learn of God to suffer long and be kind, to bear all things, and hope all things.

* So Ewald and Delitzsch. † Hupfeld.
‡ Perowne.

Of these psalms the xxii. is remarkable. In it David's personal experience seems to afford only the starting-point for a purely Messianic prophecy, which embraces many particulars that far transcend anything recorded of his sorrows. The impossibility of finding occurrences in his life corresponding to such traits as tortured limbs and burning thirst, pierced hands and parted garments, has driven some critics to the hypothesis that we have here a psalm of the exile describing either actual sufferings inflicted on some unknown confessor in Babylon, or in figurative language the calamities of Israel there. But the Davidic origin is confirmed by many obvious points of resemblance with the psalms which are indisputably his, and especially with those of the Sauline period, while the difficulty of finding historical facts answering to the emphatic language is evaded, not met, by either assuming that such facts existed in some life which has left no trace, or by forcing a metaphorical sense on words which sound wonderfully like the sad language of a real sufferer. Of course, if we believe that prediction is an absurdity, any difficulty will be lighter than the acknowledgment that we have prediction here. But, unless we have a foregone conclusion of that sort to blind us, we shall see in this psalm a clear example of the prophecy of a suffering Messiah. In most of the other psalms where David speaks of his sorrows we have only a typical foreshadowing of Christ. But in this, and in such others as lxix. and cix. (if these are David's), we have type changing into prophecy, and the person of the psalmist fading away before the image which, by occasion of his own griefs, rose vast, and solemn, and distant before his prophet gaze,—the image of One who should be perfectly all which he was in partial measure, the anointed of God, the utterer of His name to His brethren, the King of Israel,—and whose path to His dominion should be thickly strewn with solitary sorrow, and reproach, and agony, to whose far more exceeding weight of woe all his affliction was light as a feather, and transitory as a moment. And when the psalmist had learned that lesson, besides all the others of trust and patience which his wanderings taught him, his schooling was nearly over, he was almost ready for a new discipline; and the slowly-evolving revelation of God's purposes, which by his sorrows had unfolded more distinctly than before "the sufferings of the Messiah," was ripening for the unveiling, in his Kinghood, of "the glory that should follow."

IX.—THE KING.

WE have now to turn and see the sudden change of fortune which lifted the exile to a throne. The heavy cloud which had brooded so long over the doomed king broke in lightning crash on the disastrous field of Gilboa. Where is there a sadder and more solemn story of the fate of a soul which makes shipwreck "of faith and of a good conscience," than that awful page which tells how, godless, wretched, mad with despair and measureless pride, he flung himself on his bloody sword, and died a suicide's death, with sons and armour-bearer and all his men, a ghastly court of corpses, laid round him? He had once been brave, modest, and kind, full of noble purposes and generous affections—and he ended so. Into what doleful regions of hate and darkness may self-will drag a soul, when once the reins fall loose from a slackened hand! And what a pathetic beam of struggling light gleams through heavy clouds, in the grateful exploit of the men of Jabesh, who remembered how he had once saved them, while yet he could care and dare for his kingdom, and perilled their lives to bear the poor headless corpse to its rude resting-place!

The news is received by the fugitive at Ziklag in striking and characteristic fashion. He first flames out in fierce wrath upon the lying Amalekite, who had hurried with the tidings and sought favour by falsely representing that he had killed the king on the field. A short shrift and a bloody end were his. And then the wrath melts into mourning. Forgetting the mad hatred and wild struggles of that poor soul, and his own wrongs, remembering only the friendship and nobleness of his earlier days, he casts over the mangled corpses of Saul and Jonathan the mantle of his sweet elegy, and bathes them with the healing waters of his unstinted praise and undying love. Not till these two offices of justice and affection had been performed, does he remember himself and the change in his own position which had been effected. He had never thought of Saul as standing between him and the kingdom; the first feeling on his death was not, as it would have been with a less devout and less generous heart, a flush of gladness at the thought of the empty throne, but a sharp pang of pain from the sense of an empty heart. And even when he begins to look forward to his own new course, there is that same remarkable passiveness which we have observed already. His first step is to "inquire of the Lord, saying, Shall I go up to any of the cities of Judah?" (2 Sam. ii. 1). He will do nothing in this crisis of his fortunes, when all which had been so long a hope seemed to be rapidly becoming a fact, until his Shepherd shall lead him. Rapid and impetuous as he was by nature, schooled to swift decisions, followed by still swifter action, knowing that a blow struck at once, while all was chaos and despair at home, might set him on the throne, he holds nature and policy and the impatience of his people in check to hear what God will say. So fully did he fulfil the vow of his early psalm, "My strength! upon thee will I wait" (lix. 9).

We can fancy the glad march to the ancient Hebron, where the great fathers of the nation lay in their rock-hewn tombs. Even before the death of Saul, David's strength had been rapidly increasing, by a constant stream of fugitives from the confusion and misery into which the kingdom had fallen. Even Benjamin, Saul's own tribe, sent him some of its famous archers—a sinister omen of the king's waning fortunes; the hardy half-independent men of Manasseh and Gad, from the pastoral uplands on the east of Jordan, "whose faces," according to the vivid description of the chronicler (1 Chron. xii. 8), "were like the faces of lions, and were as swift as roes upon the mountains," sought his standard; and from his own kinsmen of Judah recruits "day by day came to David to help him, until it was a great host like the host of God." With such forces, it would have been child's play to have subdued any scattered troops of the former dynasty which might still have been in a condition to keep the field. But he made no attempt of the sort; and even when he came to Hebron he took no measures to advance any claims to the crown. The language of the history seems rather to imply a disbanding of his army, or at least their settling down to domestic life in the villages round Hebron, without a thought of winning the kingdom by arms. And his elevation to the partial monarchy which he at first possessed was the spontaneous act of "the men of Judah," who come to him and anoint him king over Judah.

The limits of his territory are substantially those of the kingdom over which his descendants ruled after Jeroboam's revolt, thus indicating the existence of a natural "line of cleavage" between north and south. The geographical position of Benjamin finally attached it to the latter monarchy; but for the present, the wish to retain the supremacy which it had had while the king was one of the tribe, made it the nucleus of a feeble and lingering opposition to David, headed by Saul's cousin Abner, and rallying round his incompetent son Ishbosheth.*
The chronology of this period is obscure. David reigned in Hebron seven years and a half, and as Ishbosheth's phantom sovereignty only occupied two of these years, and those evidently the last, it would appear almost as if

---

* The Canaanitish worship of Baal seems to have lingered in Saul's family. One of his grand-uncles was named Baal (1 Chron. ix. 36); his son was really called Eshbaal (Fire of Baal), which was contemptuously converted into Ishbosheth (Man of Shame). So also Mephibosheth was properly Meribbaal (Fighter for Baal).

the Philistines had held the country, with the exception of Judah, in such force that no rival cared to claim the dangerous dignity, and that five years passed before the invaders were so far cleared out as to leave leisure for civil war.

The summary narrative of these seven years presents the still youthful king in a very lovable light. The same temper which had marked his first acts after Saul's death is strikingly brought out (2 Sam. ii.—iv.) He seems to have left the conduct of the war altogether to Joab, as if he shrank from striking a single blow for his own advancement. When he does interfere, it is on the side of peace, to curb and chastise ferocious vengeance and dastardly assassination. The incidents recorded all go to make up a picture of rare generosity, of patient waiting for God to fulfil His purposes, of longing that the miserable strife between the tribes of God's inheritance should end. He sends grateful messages to Jabesh-Gilead; he will not begin the conflict with the insurgents. The only actual fight recorded is provoked by Abner, and managed with unwonted mildness by Joab. The list of his children born in Hebron is inserted in the very heart of the story of the insurrection, a token of the quiet domestic life of peaceful joys and cares which he lived while the storm was raging without. Eagerly, and without suspicion, he welcomes Abner's advances towards reconciliation. He falls for a moment to the level of his times, and yields to a strong temptation, in making the restoration of his long-lost wife Michal the condition of further negotiations—a demand which was strictly just, no doubt, but for which little more can be said. The generosity of his nature and the ideal purity of his love, which that incident shadows, shine out again in his indignation at Joab's murder of Abner, though he was too meek to avenge it. There is no more beautiful picture in his life than that of his following the bier where lay the bloody corpse of the man who had been his enemy ever since he had known him, and sealing the reconciliation which Death ever makes in noble souls, by the pathetic dirge he chanted over Abner's grave. We have a glimpse of his people's unbounded confidence in him, given incidentally when we are told that his sorrow pleased them, "as whatsoever the king did pleased all the people." We have a glimpse of the feebleness of his new monarchy as against the fierce soldier who had done so much to make it, in his acknowledgment that he was yet weak, being but recently anointed king, and that these vehement sons of Zeruiah were too strong for him; and we have a remarkable trace of connection with the psalms, in the closing words with which he invokes on Joab the vengeance which he as yet felt himself unable to execute: "The Lord shall reward the doer of evil according to his wickedness."

The only other incident recorded of his reign in Hebron is his execution of summary justice upon the murderers of the poor puppet-king Ishbosheth, upon whose death, following so closely that of Abner, the whole resistance to David's power collapses. There had never been any real popular opposition. His enemies are emphatically named as "the house of Saul," and we find Abner himself admitting that "the elders of Israel" wanted David as king (2 Sam. iii. 17), so that when he was gone, it is two Benjamites who give the *coup-de-grâce* to Ishbosheth, and end the whole shadowy rival power. Immediately the rulers of all the tribes come up to Hebron, with the tender of the crown. They offer it on the triple grounds of kinship, of his military service even in Saul's reign, and of the Divine promise of the throne. A solemn pact was made, and David was anointed in Hebron, a king by Divine right, but also a constitutional monarch chosen by popular election, and limited in his powers.

The first result of his new strength is the capture of the old hill-fortress of the Jebusites, the city of Melchizedek, which had frowned down upon Israel unsubdued till now, and whose inhabitants trusted so absolutely in its natural strength that their answer to the demand for surrender was the jeer, "Thou wilt not come hither, but the blind and lame will drive thee away." This time David does not leave the war to others. For the first time for seven years we read, "*The king* and his men went to Jerusalem." Established there as his capital, he reigns for some ten years with unbroken prosperity over a loyal and loving people, with this for the summary of the whole period, "David went on and grew great, and the Lord God of Hosts was with him" (2 Sam. v. 10). These years are marked by three principal events—the bringing up of the ark to the city of David, the promise by Nathan of the perpetual dominion of his house, and the unbroken flow of victories over the surrounding nations. These are the salient points of the narrative in the Book of Samuel (2 Sam. v.—viii.), and are all abundantly illustrated by the psalms. We shall have next then to consider "The Songs of the King."

How did the fugitive bear his sudden change of fortune? What were his thoughts when at last the dignity which he had ever expected and never sought was his? The answer is ready to our hand in that grand psalm (Ps. xviii.) which he "spake in the day that the Lord delivered him from all his enemies, and from the hand of Saul." The language of this superscription seems to connect the psalm with the period of internal and external repose which preceded and prompted David's "purpose to build an house for the Lord" (2 Sam. vii.) The same thankfulness which glows so brightly in the psalm stimulated that desire, and the emphatic reference to the mercy promised by God to "his seed for evermore," which closes the hymn, points perhaps to the definite promise of the perpetuity of the kingdom to his descendants, which was God's answer to the same desire. But whether the psalm belongs to the years of the partial sovereignty at Hebron, or to those of the complete dominion at Jerusalem, it cannot be later than the second of these two dates; and whatever may have been the time of its composition, the feelings which it expresses are those of the first freshness of thankful praise when he was firmly settled in the kingdom. Some critics would throw it onwards to the very close of his life. But this has little in its favour beyond the fact that the author of the Book of Samuel has placed his version of the psalm among the records of David's last days. There is, however, nothing to show that that position is due to chronological considerations. The victories over heathen nations which are supposed to be referred to in the psalm, and are relied on by the advocates of later date, really point to the earlier, which was the time of his most brilliant conquests. And the marked assertions of his own purity, as well as the triumphant tone of the whole, neither of which characteristics corresponds to the sad and shaded years after his great fall, point in the same direction. On the whole, then, we may fairly take this psalm as belonging to the bright beginning of the monarchy, and as showing us how well the king remembered the vows which the exile had mingled with his tears.

It is one long outpouring of rapturous thankfulness and triumphant adoration, which streams from a full heart in buoyant waves of song. Nowhere else, even in the psalms—and if not there, certainly nowhere else—is there such a continuous tide of unmingled praise, such magnificence of imagery, such passion of love to the delivering God, such joyous energy of conquering trust. It throbs throughout with the life blood of devotion. The strong flame, white with its very ardour, quivers with its own intensity as it steadily rises heavenward. All the terrors, and pains, and dangers of the weary years—the black fuel for the ruddy glow—melt into warmth too great for smoke, too equable to blaze. The plaintive notes that had so often wailed from his harp, sad as if the night wind had been wandering among its chords, have all led up to this rushing burst of full-toned gladness. The very blessedness of heaven is anticipated, when sorrows gone by are understood and seen in their connection with the joy to which they have led, and are felt to be the theme for deepest thankfulness. Thank God that, for the consolation of the whole world, we have this hymn of praise from the same lips which said, "My life is spent with grief, and my years with sighing." "We have seen the end of the Lord, that the Lord is very pitiful and of tender mercy." The tremulous minors of trustful sorrow shall swell into rapturous praise; and he who, compassed with foes, cries upon God, will, here or yonder, sing this song "unto the Lord, in the day that the Lord delivers him from the hand of all his enemies."

X.—THE KING—*CONTINUED.*

IN our last chapter we have seen that the key-note of "The Songs of the King" may be said to be struck in Psalm xviii. Its complete analysis would carry us far beyond our limits. We can but glance at some of the more prominent points of the psalm.

The first clause strikes the key-note. "I love Thee, O Jehovah, my strength." That personal attachment to God, which is so characteristic of David's religion, can no longer be pent up in silence, but gushes forth like some imprisoned stream, broad and full even from its well-head. The common word for "love" is too weak for him, and he bends to his use another, never elsewhere employed to express man's emotions towards God, the intensity of which is but feebly expressed by some such periphrasis as, "From my heart do I love Thee." The same exalted feeling is wonderfully set forth by the loving accumulation of Divine names which follow, as if he would heap together in one great pile all the rich experiences of that God, unnamed after all names, which he had garnered up in his distresses and deliverances. They tell so much as the poor vehicle of words can tell, what his Shepherd in the heavens had been to him. They are the treasures which he has brought back from his exile; and they most pathetically point to the songs of that time. He had called on God by these names when it was hard to believe in their reality, and now he repeats them all in his glad hour of fruition, for token that they who in their extremity trust in the name of the Lord will one day have the truth of faith transformed into truth of experience. "Jehovah, my rock and my fortress," reminds us of his cry in Ziklag, "Thou art my rock and my fortress" (xxxi. 3), and of the "hold" (the same word) of Adullam in which he had lain secure. "My deliverer" echoes many a sigh in the past, now changed into music of praise. "My rock" (a different word from that in a preceding clause), "in whom I take refuge," recalls the prayer, "Be Thou my rock of strength" (xxxi. 2), and his former effort of confidence, when, in the midst of calamities, he said, "My soul takes refuge in Thee" (lvii. 1.) "My shield" carries us back to the ancient promise, fresh after so many centuries, and fulfilled anew in every age, "Fear not, Abram, I am thy shield," and to his own trustful words at a time when trust was difficult, "My shield is upon God" (vii. 10). "My high tower," the last of this glowing series, links on to the hope breathed in the first song of his exile, "God is my defence" (the same expression); "Thou hast been my defence in the day of trouble" (lix. 9, 16). And then he sums up his whole past in one general sentence, which tells his habitual resource in his troubles, and the blessed help which he has ever found, "I call on Jehovah, who is worthy to be praised;* and from my enemies am I saved" (verse 3).

No comment can heighten, and no translation can adequately represent, while none can altogether destroy the unapproachable magnificence of the description which follows, of the majestic coming forth of God in answer to his cry. It stands at the very highest point, even when compared with the other sublime passages

---

* The old English word "the worshipful" comes near the form and meaning of the phrase.

of a like kind in Scripture. How pathetically he paints his sore need in metaphors which again bring to mind the songs of the outlaw :—

> The snares of death compassed me,
> And floods of destruction made me afraid ;
> The snares of Sheol surrounded me,
> The toils of death surprised me.

As he so often likened himself to some wild creature in the nets, so here Death, the hunter, has cast his fatal cords about him, and they are ready suddenly to close on the unsuspecting prey. Or, varying the image, he is sinking in black waters, which are designated by a difficult phrase (literally, "streams of Belial," or worthlessness), which is most probably rendered as above (so Ewald, Hupfeld). In this dire extremity one thing alone is left him. He is snared, but he has his voice free to cry with, and a God to cry to. He is all but sinking, but he can still shriek (so one of the words might be rendered) "like some strong swimmer in his agony." And it is enough. That one loud call for help rises, like some slender pillar of incense-smoke, straight into the palace temple of God—and, as he says, with a meaning which our version obscures, "My cry before

Him came into His ears." The prayer that springs from a living consciousness of being in God's presence, even when nearest to perishing, is the prayer that He hears. The cry is a poor, thin, solitary voice, unheard on earth, though shrill enough to rise to heaven; the answer shakes creation. One man in his extremity can put in motion all the magnificence of God. Overwhelming is the contrast between the cause and the effect. And marvellous as the greatness, so also is the swiftness of the answer. A moment suffices—and then! Even whilst he cries, the rocking earth and the quivering foundations of the hills are conscious that the Lord comes from afar for his help. The majestic self-revelation of God as the deliverer has for its occasion the psalmist's cry of distress, and for its issue, "He drew me out of many waters." All the splendour flames out because a poor man prays, and all the upheaval of earth and the artillery of heaven has simply this for its end, that a poor man may be delivered. The paradox of prayer never found a more bold expression than in this triumphant utterance, of the insignificant occasion for, and the equally insignificant result sought by, the exercise of the energy of Omnipotence.

The Divine deliverance is set forth under the familiar image of the coming of God in a tempest. Before it bursts, and simultaneous with the prayer, the "earth rocks and quivers," the sunless "pillars of the hills reel and rock to and fro," as if conscious of the gathering wrath which begins to flame far off in the highest heavens. There has been no forth-putting yet of the Divine power. It is but accumulating its fiery energy, and already the solid framework of the world trembles, anticipating the coming crash. The firmest things shake, the loftiest bow before His wrath. "There went up smoke out of his nostrils, and fire out of his mouth devoured; coals were kindled by it." This kindling anger, expressed by these tremendous metaphors, is conceived of as the preparation in "His temple" for the earthly manifestation of delivering vengeance. It is like some distant thunder-cloud which grows on the horizon into ominous blackness, and seems to be filling its ashen-coloured depths with store of lightnings. Then the piled-up terror begins to move, and, drawing nearer, pours out an avalanche of gloom seamed with fire. First the storm-cloud descends, hanging lower and lower in the sky. And whose foot is that which is planted upon its heavy mass, thick and frowning enough to be the veil of God?

> "He bowed the heavens, and came down,
> And blackness of cloud was under His feet."

Then the sudden rush of wind which heralds the lightning breaks the awful silence :—

> And He rode upon a cherub, and did fly,
> Yea, He swept along upon the wings of the wind.

The cherubs bear, as in a chariot, the throned God, and the swift pinions of the storm bear the cherubs. But He that sits upon the throne, above material forces and the highest creatures, is unseen. The psalmist's imagination stops at its base, nor dares to gaze into that light above; and the silence is more impressive than all words. Instead of pagan attempts at a likeness of God, we have next painted, with equal descriptive accuracy, poetic force, and theological truth, the pitchy blackness which hides Him. In the gloom of its depths He makes His "secret place" His "tent." It is "darkness of waters," that is, darkness from which streams out the thunder-rain; it is "thick clouds of the skies;" or perhaps the expression should be rendered, "heavy masses of clouds." Then comes the crash of the tempest. The brightness that lies closer around Him, and lives in the heart of the blackness, flames forth, parting the thick clouds —and through the awful rent hail and coals of fire are flung down on the trembling earth. The grand description may be rendered in two ways: either that adopted in our version, "At the brightness that was before Him His thick clouds passed—hailstones and coals of fire;" or, "Through His thick clouds there passed hailstones and coals of fire." The former of these is the more dramatic; the broken construction expresses more vividly the fierce suddenness of the lightning blaze and of the downrush of the hail, and is confirmed by the repetition of the same words in the same construction in the next verse. That verse describes another burst of the tempest—the deep roll of the thunder along the skies is the voice of Jehovah, and again the lightning tears through the clouds, and the hail streams down. With what profound truth all this destructive power is represented as coming from the brightness of

God—that "glory" which in its own nature is light, but in its contact with finite and sinful creatures must needs become darkness, rent asunder by lightning! What lessons as to the root and the essential nature of all punitive acts of God cluster round such words! and how calm and blessed the faith which can pierce even the thickest mass "that veileth Love!"— to see the light at the centre, even though the circumference be brooding thunder-clouds torn by sudden fires. Then comes the purpose of all this apocalypse of Divine magnificence. The fiery arrows scatter the psalmist's enemies. The waters in which he had well nigh drowned are dried up before the hot breath of His anger. "That dread voice" speaks "which shrinks their streams." And amid the blaze of tempest, the rocking earth, and the failing floods, His arm is thrust forth from above, and draws His servant from many waters. As one in later times, "he was afraid, and beginning to sink, he cried, saying, Lord, save me; and immediately He stretched forth His hand and caught him."

A calmer tone follows, as the psalmist recounts without metaphor his deliverance, and reiterates the same assertion of his innocence which we have already found so frequently in the previous psalms (vers. 17—24). Rising from his personal experience to the broad and lofty thoughts of God which that experience had taught him, as it does all who prize life chiefly as a means of knowing Him, he proclaims the solemn truth, that in the exercise of a righteous retribution, and by the very necessity of our moral nature, God appears to man what man is to God: loving to the loving, upright to the upright, pure to the pure, and froward to the froward. Our thoughts of God are shaped by our moral character; the capacity of perceiving depends on sympathy. "Unless the eye were light, how could it see the sun?" The self-revelation of God in His providence, of which only the psalm speaks, is modified according to our moral character, being full of love to those who love, being harsh and antagonistic to those who set themselves in opposition to it. There is a higher law of grace, whereby the sinfulness of man but draws forth the tenderness of a father's pardoning pity; and the brightest revelation of His love is made to froward prodigals. But that is not in the psalmist's view here, nor does it interfere with the law of retribution in its own sphere.

The purely personal tone is again resumed, and continued unbroken to the close. In the former portion David was passive, except for the voice of prayer, and God's arm alone was his deliverance. In the latter half he is active, the conquering king, whose arm is strengthened for victory by God. This difference may possibly suggest the reference of the former half to the Sauline persecution, when, as we have seen, the exile ever shrunk from avenging himself; and of the latter to the early years of his monarchy, which, as we shall see, were characterized by much successful military activity; and if so, the date of the psalm would most naturally be taken to be the close of his victorious campaigns, when "the Lord had given him rest from all his enemies round about" (2 Sam. vii. 1). Be that as it may, the latter portion of the psalm shows us the soldier king tracing all his past victories to God alone, and building upon them the confidence of a worldwide dominion. The point at which memory passes into hope is difficult to determine, and great variety of opinion prevails on the matter among commentators. It is perhaps best to follow many of the older versions, and the valuable exposition of Hupfeld, in regarding the whole section from ver. 37 of our translation as the expression of the trust which past experience had wrought. We shall then have two periods in the second half of the psalm—the past victories won by God's help (vers. 31—36), the coming triumphs of which these are the pledge (vers. 37—end).

In the former there shine out not only David's habitual consciousness of dependence on and aid from God, but also a very striking picture of his physical qualifications for a military leader. He is girded with bodily strength, swift and sure of foot like a deer, able to scale the crags where his foes fortified themselves like the wild antelopes he had so often seen bounding among the dizzy ledges of the cliffs in the wilderness; his hands are trained for war, and his sinewy arms can bend the great bow of brass. But these capacities are gifts, and not they, but their Giver, have made him victorious. Looking back upon all his past, this is its summing up :—

> "Thou hast also given me the shield of Thy salvation,
> And Thy right hand hath holden me up,
> And Thy loveliness hath made me great."

God's strength, God's buckler, God's supporting hand, God's condescension, by which He bows down to look upon and help the feeble, with the humble showing Himself humble—these have been his weapons, and from these has come his victory.

And because of these, he looks forward to a future like the past, but more glorious still, thereby teaching us how the unchanging faithfulness of our God should encourage us to take all the blessings which we have received as but the earnest of what is yet to come. He sees himself pursuing his enemies, and smiting them to the ground. The fierce light of battle blazes through the rapid sentences which paint the panic flight, and the swift pursuit, the vain shrieks to man and God for succour, and the utter annihilation of the foe:—

> (42) "And I will pound them like dust before the wind,
> Like street-filth will I empty them out."

Then he gives utterance to the consciousness that his kingdom is destined to extend far beyond the limits of Israel, in words which, like so many of the prophecies, may be translated in the present tense, but are obviously future in signification—the prophet placing himself in imagination in the midst of the time of which he speaks:—

(43) "Thou deliverest me from the strivings of the people (*i.e.*, Israel),
Thou makest me head of the heathen;
People whom I knew not serve me.

(44) At the hearing of the ear they obey me.
The sons of the stranger feign obedience to me.

(45) The sons of the stranger fade away,
They come trembling from their hiding-places."

The rebellion which weakened his early reign is subdued, and beyond the bounds of his own people his dominion spreads. Strange tribes submit to the very sound of his name, and crouch before him in extorted and pretended submission. The words are literally "lie unto me," descriptive of the profuse professions of loyalty characteristic of conquered orientals. Their power withers before him like a gathered flower before a hot wind, and the fugitives creep trembling out of their holes where they have hid themselves.

Again he recurs to the one thought which flows like a river of light through all the psalm —that all his help is in God. The names which he lovingly heaped together at the beginning are in part echoed in the close. "The Lord liveth, and blessed is my rock, and the God of my salvation is exalted." His deliverances have taught him to know a living God, swift to hear, active to help, in whom he lives, who has magnified His own name in that He has saved His servant. And as that blessed conviction is the sum of all his experience, so one glad vow expresses all his resolves, and thrills with the expectation which he had cherished even in his lonely exile, that the music of his psalm would one day echo through all the world. With lofty consciousness of his new dignity, and with lowly sense that it is God's gift, he emphatically names himself *His king*, *His* anointed, taking, as it were, his crown from his brows and laying it on the altar. With prophetic eye he looks onward, and sees the throne to which he had been led by a series of miracles enduring for ever, and the mercy of God sustaining the dominion of his house through all generations:—

(49) "Therefore will I give thanks to Thee among the nations, O Jehovah,
And to Thy name will I strike the harp:

(50) Who maketh great the deliverances of His king,
And executeth mercy for His anointed,
For David and his seed for evermore."

And what were his purposes for the future? Here is his answer, in a psalm which has been with considerable appropriateness regarded as a kind of manifesto of the principles which he intended should characterize his reign (Psa. ci.): "I will walk within my house with a perfect heart. I will set no wicked thing before mine eyes." For himself, he begins his reign with noble self-restraint, not meaning to make it a region of indulgence, but feeling that there is a law above his will, of which he is only the servant, and knowing that if his people and his public life are to be what they should be, his own personal and domestic life must be pure. As for his court and his ministers, he will make a clean sweep of the vermin who swarm and sting and buzz about a throne. The froward, the wicked, privy slanderers, proud hearts, crafty plotters, liars, and evil-doers he will not suffer—but "mine eyes shall be upon the faithful in the land; he that walketh in a perfect way, he shall serve me." He is fired with ambition, such as has brightened the beginning of many a reign which has darkened to cruelty and crime, to make his kingdom some faint image of God's, and to bring the actual Israel into conformity with its ancient Magna Charta, "Ye shall be to me a holy nation." And so, not knowing perhaps how hard a task he planned, and little dreaming of his own sore fall, he grasps the sword, resolved to use it for the terror of evil-doers, and vows, "I will early destroy all the wicked in the land, that I may cut off all wicked doers from the city of the Lord." Such was his "proclamation against vice and immorality" on his accession to his throne.

XI.—THE KING—*CONTINUED.*

THE years thus well begun are, in the historical books, characterized mainly by three events, namely, the bringing up of the ark to the newly won city of David, Nathan's prophecy of the perpetual dominion of his house, and his victories over the surrounding nations. These three hinges of the narrative are all abundantly illustrated in the psalms.

As to the first, we have relics of the joyful ceremonial connected with it in two psalms, the fifteenth and twenty-fourth, which are singularly alike not only in substance but in manner, both being thrown into a highly dramatic form by question and answer. This peculiarity, as we shall see, is one of the links of connection which unite them with the history as given in the Book of Samuel (2 Sam. vi.). From that record we learn that David's first thought after he was firmly seated as king over all Israel, was the enthronement in his recently-captured city of the long-forgotten ark. That venerable symbol of the presence of the true King had passed through many vicissitudes since the days when it had been carried round the walls of Jericho. Superstitiously borne into battle, as if it were a mere magic palladium, by men whose hearts were not right with God, the presence which they had invoked became their ruin, and Israel was shattered, and "the ark of God taken," on the fatal field of Aphek. It had been carried in triumph through Philistine cities, and sent back in dismay. It had been welcomed with gladness by the villagers of Bethshemesh, who lifted their eyes from their harvest work, and saw it borne up the glen from the Philistine plain. Their rude curiosity was signally punished, "and the men of Bethshemesh said, Who is able to stand before this holy Lord God, and to whom shall He go up from us?" It had been removed to the forest seclusion of Kirjath-jearim (the city of the woods), and there bestowed in the house of Abinadab "upon the hill," where it lay neglected and forgotten for about seventy years. During Saul's reign they "inquired not at it," and, indeed, the whole worship of Jehovah seems to have been decaying. David set himself to reorganize the public service of God, arranged a staff of priests and Levites, with disciplined choir and orchestra (1 Chron. xv.), and then proceeded with representatives of the whole nation to bring up the ark from its woodland hiding-place. But again death turned gladness into dread, and Uzzah's fate silenced the joyous songs, "and David was afraid of the Lord that day, and said, How shall the ark of God come unto me?" The dangerous honour fell on the house of Obed-edom; and only after the blessing which followed its three months' stay there, did he venture to carry out his purpose. The story of the actual removal of the ark to the city of David with glad ceremonial need not be repeated here; nor the mocking gibes of Michal who had once loved him so fondly. Probably she bitterly resented her violent separation from the household joys that had grown up about her in her second home; probably the woman who had had teraphim among her furniture cared nothing for the ark of God; probably, as she grew older, her character had hardened in its lines, and become like her father's in its measureless pride, and in its half-dread, half-hatred of David—and all these motives together pour their venom into her sarcasm. Taunts provoke taunts; the husband feels that the wife is in heart a partisan of the fallen house of her father, and a despiser of the Lord and of His worship; her words hiss with scorn, his flame with anger and rebuke—and so these two that had been so tender in the old days part for ever. The one doubtful act that stained his accession was quickly avenged. Better for both that she had never been rent from that feeble, loving husband that followed her weeping, and was driven back by a single word, flung at him by Abner as if he had been a dog at their heels! (2 Sam. iii. 16).

The gladness and triumph, the awe, and the memories of victory which clustered round the dread symbol of the presence of the Lord of Hosts, are wonderfully expressed in the choral twenty-fourth psalm. It is divided into two portions, which Ewald regards as being originally two independent compositions. They are, however, obviously connected both in form and substance. In each we have question and answer, as in psalm xv., which belongs to the same period. The first half replies to the question, "Who shall ascend the hill of the

Lord, and who shall stand in His holy place?"—an echo of the terror-struck exclamation of the people of Bethshemesh, already quoted. The answer is a description of the *men who dwell with God.* The second half deals with the correlative inquiry, "Who is the King of Glory?" and describes the *God who comes to dwell with men.* It corresponds in substance, though not in form, with David's thought when Uzzah died, in so far as it regards God as drawing near to the worshippers, rather than the worshippers drawing near to Him. Both portions are united by a real internal connection, in that they set forth the mutual approach of God and man which leads to communion, and thus constitute the two halves of an inseparable whole.

Most expositors recognise a choral structure in the psalm, as in several others of this date, as would be natural at the time of the reorganization of the public musical service. Probably we may gain the key to its form by supposing it to be a processional hymn, of which the first half was to be sung during the ascent to the city of David, and the second while standing before the gates. We have then to fancy the long line of worshippers climbing the rocky steep hill-side to the ancient fortress so recently won, the Levites bearing the ark, and the glad multitude streaming along behind them.

First there swells forth from all the singers the triumphant proclamation of God's universal sovereignty, "The earth is the Lord's and the fulness thereof; the world and they that dwell therein. For He hath founded it upon the seas and established it upon the floods." It is very noteworthy that such a thought should precede the declaration of His special dwelling in Zion. It guards that belief from the abuses to which it was of course liable—the superstitions, the narrowness, the contempt of all the rest of the world as God-deserted, which are its perversion in sensuous natures. If Israel came to fancy that God belonged to them, and that there was only one sacred place in all the world, it was not for want of clear utterances to the contrary, which became more emphatic with each fresh step in the development of the specializing system under which they lived. The very ground of their peculiar relation to God had been declared, in the hour of constituting it to be—"all the earth is Mine" (Exod. xix. 5). So now, when the symbol of His presence is to have a local habitation in the centre of the national life, the psalmist lays for the foundation of his song the great truth, that the Divine presence is concentrated in Israel, but not confined there, and concentrated in order that it may be diffused. The glory that lights the bare top of Zion lies on all the hills; and He who dwells between the cherubim dwells in all the world, which His continual presence fills with its fulness, and upholds above the floods.

Then, as they climb, a single voice perhaps chants the solemn question, "Who shall ascend the hill of the Lord, or who shall stand in the place of His holiness?"

And the full-toned answer portrays the men who shall dwell with God, in words which begin indeed with stringent demands for absolute purity, but wonderfully change in tone as they advance, into gracious assurances, and the clearest vision that the moral nature which fits for God's presence is God's gift. "The clean-handed, and pure-hearted, who has not lifted up his soul to vanity, nor sworn deceitfully;" there is the eternal law which nothing can ever alter, that to abide with God a man must be like God—the law of the new covenant as of the old, "Blessed are the pure in heart, for they shall see God." But this requirement, impossible of fulfilment, is not all. If it were, the climbing procession might stop. But up and up they rise, and once again the song bursts forth in deeper and more hopeful words, " He shall *receive* the blessing from Jehovah, and righteousness from the God of his salvation." Then that righteousness, which he who honestly attempts to comply with such requirements will soon find that he does not possess, is to be received from above, not elaborated from within; is a gift from God, not a product of man's toils. God will make us pure, that we may dwell with Him. Nor is this all. The condition of receiving such a gift has been already partially set forth in the preceding clause, which seems to require righteousness to be possessed as the preliminary to receiving it. The paradox which thus results is inseparable from the stage of religious knowledge attained under the Mosaic Law. But the last words of the answer go far beyond it, and proclaim the special truth of the gospel, that the righteousness which fits for dwelling with God is given on the simple condition of *seeking* Him. To this designation of the true worshippers is appended somewhat abruptly the one word "Jacob," which need neither be rendered as in the English version as an invocation, nor as in the margin, with an unnecessary and improbable supplement, "O God of Jacob;" but is best regarded as in apposition with the other descriptive clauses, and declaring, as we have found David doing already in previous psalms, that the characters portrayed in them, and these only, constituted the true Israel.

> This is the generation of them that seek Him,
> That seek Thy face—(this is) Jacob.

And so the first question is answered, "Who are the men who dwell with God?"—The pure, who receive righteousness, who seek Him, the true Israel.

And now the procession has reached the front of the ancient city on the hill, and stands before the very walls and weather-beaten gates which Melchizedek may have passed through, and which had been barred against Israel till David's might had burst them. National triumph and glad worship are wonderfully blended in the summons which rings from the lips of the Levites without: "Lift up your heads, O ye gates! and be ye lift up, ye doors (that have been from) of old!" as if even their towering portals were too low, "and the King of glory shall come in." What force in that name here, in this early song of the King! How clearly he recognises his own derived power, and the real Monarch of whom he is but the shadowy representative! The newly-conquered city is summoned to admit its true conqueror and sovereign, whose throne is the ark, which was emphatically named "the glory,"* and in whose train the earthly king follows as a subject and a worshipper. Then, with wonderful dramatic force, a single voice from within the barred gates asks, like some suspicious warder, "Who then is the King of glory?" With what a shout of proud confidence and triumphant memories of a hundred fields comes, ready and full, the crash of many voices in the answer, "Jehovah strong and mighty, Jehovah mighty in battle!" How vividly the reluctance of an antagonistic world to yield to Israel and Israel's King, is represented in the repetition of the question in a form slightly more expressive of

* "And she named the child I-chabod (Where is the glory?) saying, The glory is departed from Israel: because the ark of God was taken."—1 *Sam.* iv. 21.

ignorance and doubt, in answer to the reiterated summons, "Who is He, then, the King of glory?" With what deepened intensity of triumph there peals, hoarse and deep, the choral shout, "The Lord of Hosts, He is the King of glory." That name which sets Him forth as Sovereign of the personal and impersonal forces of the universe —angels, and stars, and terrene creatures, all gathered in ordered ranks, embattled for His service—was a comparatively new name in Israel,* and brought with it thoughts of irresistible might in earth and heaven. It crashes like a catapult against the ancient gates; and at that proclamation of the omnipotent name of the God who dwells with men, they grate back on their brazen hinges, and the ark of the Lord enters into its rest.

* It has been asserted that this is the first introduction of the name. ("Psalms Chronologically Arranged by Four Friends," p. 14). But it occurs in Hannah's vow (1 Sam. i. 11): in Samuel's words to Saul (xv. 2); in David's reply to Goliath (xvii. 45). We have it also in Psalm lix. 5, which we regard as his earliest during his exile. Do the authors referred to consider these speeches in 1 Sam. as not authentic?

XII.—THE KING—*CONTINUED*.

THE second event recorded as important in the bright early years is the great promise of the perpetuity of the kingdom in David's house. As soon as the king was firmly established and free from war, he remembered the ancient word which said, "When He giveth you rest from all your enemies round about, so that ye dwell in safety, then there shall be a place which the Lord your God shall choose to cause His name to dwell there" (Deut. xii. 10, 11). His own ease rebukes him; he regards his tranquillity not as a season for selfish indolence, but as a call to new forms of service. He might well have found in the many troubles and vicissitudes of his past life an excuse for luxurious repose now. But devout souls will consecrate their leisure as their toil to God, and will serve Him with thankful offerings in peace whom they invoked with earnest cries in battle. Prosperity is harmless only when it is accepted as an opportunity for fresh forms of devotion, not as an occasion for idle self-indulgence. So we read, with distinct verbal reference to the words already quoted, that "when the Lord had given him rest round about from all his enemies, the king said unto Nathan the prophet, See now, I dwell in an house of cedar, but the ark of God dwelleth in curtains." The impulse of generous devotion, which cannot bear to lavish more upon self than it gives to God, at first commended itself to the prophet; but in the solitude of his nightly thoughts the higher wisdom speaks in his spirit, and the word of God gives him a message for the king. The narrative in 2 Sam. makes no mention of David's warlike life as unfitting him for the task, which we find from 2 Chron. was one reason why his purpose was set aside, but brings into prominence the thought that David's generous impulse was outrunning God's commandment, and that his ardour to serve was in some danger of forgetting his entire dependence on God, and of fancying that God would be the better for him. So the prophetic message reminds him that the Lord had never, through all the centuries, asked for a house of cedar, and recalls the past life of David as having been wholly shaped and blessed by Him, while it pointedly inverts the king's proposal in its own grand promise, "The Lord telleth thee that He will make thee an house." Then follows the prediction of a son of David who should build the house, whose kingdom should be perpetual, whose transgressions should be corrected indeed, but never punished as those of the unhappy Saul; and then, in emphatic and unmistakable words, the perpetuity of David's house, his kingdom, and his throne, is reiterated as the close of the whole.

The wonderful burst of praise which sprang from David's heart in answer cannot be dealt with here; but clearly from that time onwards a new element had been added to his hopes, and a new object presented to his faith. The prophecy of the Messiah enters upon a new stage, bearing a relation, as its successive stages, always unmistakably did, to the history which supplies a framework for it. Now for the first time can he be set forth as the king of Israel; now the width of the promise which at first had embraced the seed of the woman, and then had been narrowed to the seed of Abraham, and thereafter probably to the tribe of Judah, is still further defined as to be fulfilled in the line of the house of David; now the personal Messiah Himself begins to be discerned through the words which are to have a preparatory fulfilment, in itself prophetic, in the collective Davidic monarchs whose very office is itself also a prophecy.

Many echoes of this new message ring through the later psalms of the king. His own dominion, his conquests, and his office, gradually became to himself a solemn prophecy of a mysterious descendant who should be really and fully all that he was in shadow and in part. As the experience of the exile, so that of the victorious monarch supplied the colours with which the spirit of prophecy in him painted "beforehand the sufferings of Christ and the glory that should follow." In both classes of psalms we have two forms of the Messianic reference, the typical and the purely prophetic. In the former the events of David's own biography and the feelings of his own soul are so portrayed and expressed as to suggest his greater Son. In the latter, the personality of the psalmist retreats into the background, and is at most only the starting-point for wails of sorrow or gleams of glory which far transcend anything in the life of the singer. There are portions, for instance, of the xxii. and lxix. psalms which no torturing can force into correspondence with any of David's trials; and in like manner there are pæans of victory and predictions of dominion which demand a grander interpretation than his own royalty or his hopes for his house can yield. Of course, if prophecy is impossible, there is no more to be said, but that in that case a considerable part of the Old Testament, including many of David's psalms, is unintelligible.

Perhaps the clearest instance of distinct prophecy of the victorious dominion of the personal Messiah is the 110th psalm. In it we do see, no doubt, the influence of the psalmist's own history, shaping the image which rises before his soul. But the attributes of that king whom he beholds are not his attributes, nor those of any son of his who wore the crown in Israel. And whilst his own history gives the form, it is "the Spirit of Christ that was in" him which gives the substance, and transfigures the earthly monarchy into a heavenly dominion. We do not enter upon the question of the Davidic authorship of this psalm. Here we have not to depend upon Jewish superscriptions, but on the words of Him whose bare assertion should be "an end of all strife." Christ says that David wrote it. Some of us are far enough behind the age to believe that what He said He meant, and that what He meant is truth.

This psalm, then, being David's, can hardly be earlier than the time of Nathan's prophecy. There are traces in it of the influence of the history of the psalmist, giving, as we have said, form to the predictions. Perhaps we may see these in Zion being named as the seat of Messiah's sovereignty and in the reference to Melchizedek, both of which points assume new force if we suppose that the ancient city over which that half-forgotten name once ruled had recently become his own. Possibly, too, his joy in exchanging his armour and kingly robe for the priest's ephod, when he brought up the ark to its rest, and his consciousness that in himself the regal and the sacerdotal offices did not blend, may have led him to meditations on the meaning of both, on the miseries that seemed to flow equally from their separation and from their union, which were the precursors of his hearing the Divine oath that, in the far-off future, they would be fused together in that mighty figure who was to repeat in higher fashion the union of functions which invested that dim King of Righteousness and Priest of God in the far-off past. He discerns that *his* support from the right hand of God, *his* sceptre which he swayed in Zion, *his* loyal people fused together into a unity at last, *his* triumphant warfare on the nations around, are all but faint shadows of One who is to come. That solemn form on the horizon of hope is his Lord, the true King whose viceroy he was, the "bright consummate flower" for the sake of which the root has its being. And, as he sees the majestic lineaments shimmering through the facts of his own history, like some hidden fire toiling in a narrow space ere it leaps into ruddy spires that burst their bonds and flame heaven high, he is borne onwards by the prophetic impulse, and the Spirit of God speaks through his tongue words which have no meaning unless their theme be a Divine ruler and priest for all the world.

He begins with the solemn words with which a prophetic message is wont to be announced, thus at the outset stamping on the psalm its true character. The "oracle" or "word of Jehovah unto my Lord," which he heard, is a new revelation made to him from the heavens. He is taken up and listens to the Divine voice calling to His right hand, to the most intimate communion with Himself, and to wielding the energies of omnipotence—Him whom David knew to be his lord. And when that Divine voice ceases, its mandate having been fulfilled, the prophetic spirit in the seer hymns the coronation anthem of the monarch enthroned by the side of the majesty in the heavens. "The sceptre of Thy strength will Jehovah send out of Zion. Rule Thou in the midst of Thine enemies." In singular juxtaposition are the throne at God's right hand and the sceptre —the emblem of sovereignty—issuing from Zion, a dominion realised on earth by a monarch in the heavens, a dominion the centre of which is Zion, and the undefined extent universal. It is a monarchy, too, established in the midst of enemies, sustained in spite of antagonism not only by the power of Jehovah, but by the activity of the sovereign's own "rule." It is a dominion for the maintenance of which devout souls will burst into prayer, and the most powerful can bring but their aspirations. But the vision includes more than the warrior king and his foes. Imbedded, as it were, in the very heart of the description of the former comes the portraiture of his subjects, for a witness how close is the union between Him and them, and how inseparable from His glories are those who serve Him. They are characterised in a threefold manner. "Thy people (shall be) willing in the day of Thine array." The army is being mustered.* They are not mercenaries, nor pressed men. They flock gladly to the standard, like the warriors celebrated of old in Deborah's chant of victory, who "willingly offered themselves." The word of our psalm might be translated "freewill offerings," and the whole clause carries us into the very heart of that great truth, that glad consecration and grateful self-surrender is the one bond which knits us to the Captain of our salvation who

---

* The word translated "power" in our version, has the same double meaning as that has in old English, or as "force" has now, sometimes signifying "strength" and sometimes an "army." The latter is the more appropriate here. "The day of Thine army" will then be equivalent to the day of mustering the troops.

gave Himself for us, to the meek Monarch whose crown is of thorns and His sceptre a reed, for tokens that His dominion rests on suffering and is wielded in gentleness. The next words should be punctuated as a separate clause, co-ordinate with the former, and adding another feature to the description of the army. "In the beauties of holiness" is a common name for the dress of the priests: the idea conveyed is that the army is an army of priests, as the king himself is a priest. They are clothed, not in mail and warlike attire, but in "fine linen clean and white," like the armies which a later prophet saw following the Lord of lords. Their warfare is not to be by force and cruelty, nor their conquests bloody; but while soldiers they are to be priests, their weapons purity and devotion, their merciful struggle to bring men to God, and to mirror God to men. Round the one image gather all ideas of discipline, courage, consecration to a cause, loyalty to a leader; round the other, all thoughts of gentleness, of an atmosphere of devotion calm and still as the holy place, of stainless character. Christ's servants must be both soldiers and priests, like some of those knightly orders who bore the cross on helmet and shield, and shaped the very hilts of their swords into its likeness. And these soldier-priests are described by yet another image, "From the womb of the morning thou hast the dew of thy youth," where we are to regard the last word as used in a collective sense, and equivalent to "Thy young warriors." They are like the dew sparkling in infinite globelets on every blade of grass, hanging gems on every bit of dead wood, formed in secret silence, reflecting the sunlight, and, though the single drops be small and feeble, yet together freshening the thirsty world. So, formed by an unseen and mysterious power, one by one insignificant, but in the whole mighty, mirroring God and quickening and beautifying the worn world, the servants of the priest-king are to be "in the midst of many people like the dew from the Lord."

Another solemn word from the lips of God begins the second half of the psalm. "Jehovah swears," gives the sanction and guarantee of His own nature, puts in pledge His own being for the fulfilment of the promise. And that which He swears is a new thing in the earth. The blending of the royal and priestly offices in the Messiah, and the eternal duration in Him of both, is a distinct advancement in the development of Messianic prophecy. The historical occasion for it may indeed be connected with David's kingship and conquest of Melchizedek's city; but the real source of it is a direct predictive inspiration. We have here not merely the devout psalmist meditating on the truths revealed before his day, but the prophet receiving a new word from God unheard by mortal ears, and far transcending even the promises made to him by Nathan. There is but one person to whom it can apply, who sits as a priest upon his throne, who builds the temple of the Lord (Zech. vi. 12, 13).

As the former Divine word, so this is followed by the prophet's rapturous answer, which carries on the portraiture of the priest-king. There is some doubt as to the person addressed in these later verses. "The Lord at thy right hand crushes kings in the day of His wrath." Whose right hand? The answer generally given is, "The Messiah's." Who is the Lord that smites the petty kinglets of earth? The answer generally given is, "God." But it is far more dramatic, avoids an awkward abruptness in the change of persons in the last verse, and brings out a striking contrast with the previous half, if we take the opposite view, and suppose Jehovah addressed and the Messiah spoken of throughout. Then the first Divine word is followed by the prophetic invocation of the exalted Messiah throned at the right hand and expecting till His enemies be made His footstool. The second is followed by the prophetic invocation of Jehovah, and describes the Lord Messiah at God's right hand as before, but instead of longer waiting He now flames forth in all the resistless energy of a conqueror. The day of His array is succeeded by the day of His wrath. He crushes earth's monarchies. The psalmist's eye sees the whole earth one great battle-field. "(It is) full of corpses. He wounds the head over wide lands," where there may possibly be a reference to the first vague dawning of a hope which God's mercy had let lighten on man's horizon—"He shall bruise thy head," or the word may be used as a collective expression for rulers, as the parallelism with the previous verse requires. Thus striding on to victory across the prostrate foe, and pursuing the flying relics of their power, "He drinks of the brook in the way, therefore shall He lift up the head," words which are somewhat difficult, however interpreted. If, with the majority of modern commentators, we take them as a picturesque embodiment of eager haste in the pursuit, the conqueror "faint, yet pursuing," and stooping for a moment to drink, then hurrying on with renewed strength after the fugitives, one can scarcely help feeling that such a close to such a psalm is trivial and liker the artificial play of fancy than the work of the prophetic spirit, to say nothing of the fact that there is nothing about pursuit in the psalm. If we fall back on the older interpretation, which sees in the words a prophecy of the sufferings of the Messiah who tastes death and drinks of the cup of sorrows, and therefore is highly exalted, we get a meaning which worthily crowns the psalm, but seems to break somewhat abruptly the sequence of thought, and to force the metaphor of drinking of the brook into somewhat strained parallelism with the very different New Testament images just named. But the doubt we must leave over these final words does not diminish the preciousness of this psalm as a clear, articulate prophecy from David's lips of David's Son, whom he had learned to know through the experiences and facts of his own life. He had climbed through sufferings to his throne. God had exalted him and given him victory, and surrounded him with a loyal people. But he was only a shadow; limitations and imperfections surrounded his office and weakened himself; half of the Divine counsel of peace could not be mirrored in his functions at all, and death lay ahead of him. So his glory and his feebleness alike taught him that "one mightier than" he must be coming behind him, "the latchet of whose shoes he was not worthy to unloose"—the true King of Israel, to bear witness to whom was his highest honour.

The third characteristic of the first seventeen years of David's reign is his successful wars with surrounding nations. The gloomy days of defeat and subjugation which had darkened the closing years of Saul are over now, and blow after blow falls with stunning rapidity on the amazed enemies. The narrative almost pants for breath as it tells with hurry and pride how, south, and east, and north, the "lion of the tribe of Judah" sprang from his fastness, and smote Philistia, Edom, Moab, Ammon, Amalek, Damascus, and the Syrians beyond, even to the

Euphrates; and the bounding courage of king and people, and the unity of heart and hand with which they stood shoulder to shoulder in many a bloody field, ring through the psalms of this period. Whatever higher meaning may be attached to them, their roots are firm in the soil of actual history, and they are first of all the war-songs of a nation. That being so, that they should also be inspired hymns for the church in all ages will present no difficulty nor afford any consecration to modern warfare, if the progressive character of revelation be duly kept in mind. There is a whole series of such psalms, such as xx., xxi., lx., and probably lxviii. We cannot venture in our limited space on any analysis of the last of these. It is a splendid burst of national triumph and devout praise, full of martial ardour, throbbing with lofty consciousness of God's dwelling in Israel, abounding with allusions to the ancient victories of the people, and world-wide in its anticipations of future triumph. How strange the history of its opening words has been! Through the battle smoke of how many a field they have rung! On the plains of the Palatinate, from the lips of Cromwell's Ironsides, and from the poor peasants that went to death on many a bleak moor for Christ's crown and covenant, to the Doric music of their rude chant—

> "Let God arise, and scatterèd
> Let all His enemies be;
> And let all those that do Him hate,
> Before His presence flee."

The sixtieth psalm is assigned to David after Joab's signal victory over the Edomites (2 Sam. viii.). It agrees very well with that date, though the earlier verses have a wailing tone so deep over recent disasters, so great that one is almost inclined to suppose that they come from a later hand than his. But after the first verses all is warlike energy and triumph. How the glad thought of ruling over a united people dances in the swift words, "I will rejoice, I will divide Shechem, and mete out the valley of Succoth;" he has, as it were, repeated Joshua's conquest and division of the land, and the ancient historical sites that fill a conspicuous place in the history of his great ancestor are in his power. "Gilead is mine, and Manasseh is mine, Ephraim also is the defence of my head, Judah my staff of command." He looks eastward to the woods and pastoral uplands across the Jordan, whose inhabitants had been but loosely attached to the western portion of the nation, and triumphs in knowing that Gilead and Manasseh own his sway. The foremost tribes on this side the river are to him like the armour and equipments of a conqueror; he wears the might of Ephraim, the natural head of the northern region, as his helmet, and he grasps the power of Judah as his baton of command or sceptre of kingly rule (Gen. xlix. 10).

Thus, strong in the possession of a united kingdom, his flashing eye turns to his enemies, and a stern joy, mingled with contempt, blazes up as he sees them reduced to menial offices and trembling before him. "Moab (is) my washing-basin; to Edom will I fling my shoe; because of me, Philistia, cry out" (in fear). The three ancestral foes that hung on Israel's southern border from east to west are subdued. He will make of one "a vessel of dishonour" to wash his feet, soiled with battle; he will throw his shoes to another the while, as one would to a slave to take care of; and the third, expecting a like fate, shrieks out in fear of the impending vengeance. He pants for new victories, "Who will bring me into (the) strong city?" probably the yet unsubdued Petra, hidden away in its tortuous ravine, with but one perilous path through the gorge. And at last all the triumph of victory rises to a higher region of thought in the closing words, which lay bare the secret of his strength, and breathe the true spirit of the soldier of Jehovah. "In God we shall do valiantly; and He, even He, shall tread down our enemies."

The twentieth psalm, another of these stirring war-songs, is in that choral manner which we have already seen in psalm xxiv., and the adoption of which was probably connected with David's careful organization of "the service of song." It is all ablaze with the light of battle and the glow of loyal love.

The army, ready drawn up for action, as we may fancy, prays for the king, who, according to custom, brings sacrifices and offerings before the fight. "Jehovah hear thee in the day of trouble; the name of the God of Jacob defend thee, send thee help from the sanctuary, and strengthen thee out of Zion, remember all thine offerings, and accept thy burnt sacrifice." Then, as they wave their standards in the sunshine, or plant before the ranks of each tribe its cognizance, to be defended to the death, the hoarse shout rises from the files, "In the name of our God we will set up (or wave) our banners." Then the single voice of the king speaks, rejoicing in his soldiers' devotion, which he accepts as an omen that his sacrifice has not been in vain: "Now know I that Jehovah saveth His anointed. He will hear him from the heaven of His holiness with the strength of the salvation of His right hand;" not merely from a God dwelling in Zion, according to language of the previous prayer, but from the Lord in the heavens, will the strength come. Then again the chorus of the host exclaims, as they look across the field to the chariots and cavalry of the foe—forces which Israel seldom used—" These (boast *) of chariots, and those of horses, and we, of the name of Jehovah, our God, do we boast." Ere a sword has been drawn, they see the enemy scattered. " They are brought down and fallen; and we, we are risen and stand upright." Then one earnest cry to God, one more thought of the true monarch of Israel, whom David would teach them to feel he only shadowed; and with the prayer, " Jehovah! save! Let the King hear us in the day when we cry," ringing like the long trumpet blast that sounds for the charge, they dash forth to victory!

* Lit. "make mention of" or "commemorate."

XIII.—THE TEARS OF THE PENITENT.

ADVERSITY had taught David self-restraint, had braced his soul, had driven him to grasp firmly the hand of God. And prosperity had seemed for nearly twenty years but to perfect the lessons. Gratitude had followed deliverance, and the sunshine after the rain had brought out the fragrance of devotion and the blossoms of glad songs. A good man, and still more a man of David's age at the date of his great crime, seldom falls so low, unless there has been previous, perhaps unconscious, relaxation of the girded loins, and negligence of the untrimmed lamp. The sensitive nature of the psalmist was indeed not unlikely to yield to the sudden force of such a temptation as conquered him, but we can scarcely conceive of its having done so without a previous decay of his religious life, hidden most likely from himself. And the source of that decay may probably be found in self-indulgence, fostered by ease, and by long years of command. The actual fall into sin seems to have been begun by slothful abdication of his functions as captain of Israel. It is perhaps not without bitter emphasis that the narrative introduces it by telling us that, "at the time when kings go forth to battle," David contented himself with sending his troops against Ammon, and "tarried still at Jerusalem." At all events, the story brings into sharp contrast the levy *en masse*, encamped round Rabbath, and their natural head, who had once been so ready to take his share of blows and privations, loitering behind, taking his quiet siesta in the hot hours after noon, as if there had been no soldiers of his sweltering in their armour, and rising from his bed to stroll on his palace roof, and peer into the household privacies below, as if his heart had no interest in the grim tussle going on behind the hills that he could almost see from his height, as they grew purple in the evening twilight. He has fallen to the level of an Eastern despot, and has lost his sense of the responsibilities of his office. Such loosening of the tension of his moral nature as is indicated in his absence from the field, during what was evidently a very severe as well as a long struggle, prepared the way for the dismal headlong plunge into sin.

The story is told in all its hideousness, without palliation or reserve, without comment or heightening, in that stern judicial fashion so characteristic of the Bible records of its greatest characters. Every step is narrated without a trace of softening, and without a word of emotion. Not a single ugly detail is spared. The portraiture is as vivid as ever. Bathsheba's willing complicity, her punctilious observance of ceremonial propriety while she is trampling under foot her holiest obligations; the fatal necessity which drags sin after sin, and summons up murder to hide, if it be possible, the foul form of adultery; the stinging rebuke in the conduct of Uriah, who, Hittite as he was, has a more chivalrous, not to say devout, shrinking from personal ease while his comrades and the ark are in the field, than the king has; the mean treason, the degradation implied in getting into Joab's power; the cynical plainness of the murderous letter, in which a hardened conscience names his purposed evil by its true name; the contemptuous measure of his master which Joab takes in his message, the king's indifference to the loss of his men so long as Uriah is out of the way; the solemn platitudes with which he pretends to console his tool for the check of his troops; and the hideous haste with which, after her scrupulous "mourning" for one week, Bathsheba threw herself again into David's arms;—all these particulars, and every particular an aggravation, stand out for ever, as men's most hidden evil will one day do, in the clear, unpitying, unmistakable light of the Divine record. What a story it is!

This saint of nearly fifty years of age, bound to God by ties which he rapturously felt and acknowledged, whose words have been the very breath of devotion for every devout heart, forgets his longings after righteousness, flings away the joys of Divine communion, darkens his soul, ends his prosperity, brings down upon his head for all his remaining years a cataract of calamities, and makes his name and his religion a target for the barbed sarcasms of each succeeding generation of scoffers. "All the fences and their whole array," which God's mercies and his own past had reared, "one cunning sin sweeps quite away." Every obligation of his office, as every grace of his character, is trodden under foot by the wild beast roused in his breast. As man, as king, as soldier, he is found wanting. Lust and treason, and craft and murder, are goodly companions for him who had said, "I will walk within my house with a perfect heart. I will set no wicked thing before mine eyes." Why should we dwell on the wretched story? Because it teaches us, as no other page in the history of God's church does, how the alchemy of Divine love can extract sweet perfumes of penitence and praise out of the filth of sin; and therefore, though we turn with loathing from David's sin, we have to bless God for the record of it, and for the lessons of hope that come from David's pardon.

To many a sin-tortured soul since then, the two psalms (li., xxxii.), all blotted with tears, in which he has sobbed out his penitence, have been as footsteps in a great and terrible wilderness. They are too familiar to need, and too sacred to bear, many words here, but we may briefly note some points connected with them —especially those which assist us in forming some image of the psalmist's state of mind after his transgression. It may be observed that of these two psalms, the fifty-first is evidently earlier than the thirty-second. In the former we see the fallen man struggling up out of the "horrible pit and miry clay;" in the latter he stands upon the rock, with a new song in his mouth, even the blessedness of him "whose sin is covered." It appears also that both must be dated after the sharp thrust of God's lancet which Nathan drove into his conscience, and the healing balsam of God's assurance of forgiveness which Nathan laid upon his heart. The passionate cries of the psalm are the echo of the Divine promise—the effort of his faith to grasp and keep the merciful gift of pardon. The consciousness of forgiveness is the basis of the prayer for forgiveness.

Somewhere about a year passed between the crime and the message of Nathan. And what sort of a year it was the psalms tell us. The coarse satisfactions of his sin could not long content him, as they might have done a lower type of man. Nobody buys a little passing pleasure in evil at so dear a rate, or keeps it for so short a time as a good man. He cannot make himself as others. "That which cometh into your mind shall not be at all, in that ye say, We will be as the families of the nations, which serve wood and stone." Old habits quickly reassert their force, conscience soon lifts again its solemn voice; and while worse men are enjoying the strong-flavoured meats on sin's table, the servant of God, who has been seduced to prefer them for a moment to the "light bread" from heaven, tastes them already bitter in his mouth. He may be far from true repentance, but he will very soon know remorse. Months may pass before he can feel again the calm joys of God, but disgust with himself and with his sin will quickly fill his soul. No more vivid picture of such a state has ever been drawn, than is found in the psalms of this period. They tell of sullen "silence;" dust had settled on the strings of his harp, as on helmet and sword. He will not speak to God of his sin, and there is nothing else that he can speak of. They tell of his "roaring all the day long"— the groan of anguish forced from his yet unsoftened spirit. Day and night God's heavy hand weighed him down; the consciousness of that power, whose gentleness had once holden him up, crushed, but did not melt him. Like some heated iron, its heaviness scorched as well as bruised, and his moisture—all the dew and freshness of his life—was dried up at its touch and turned into dusty, cracking drought, that chaps the hard earth, and shrinks the streamlets, and burns to brown powder the tender herbage (Ps. xxxii.). Body and mind seem both to be included in this wonderful description, in which obstinate dumbness, constant torture, dread of God, and not one softening drop of penitence fill the dry and dusty heart, while "bones waxing old," or, as the word might be rendered, "rotting," sleepless nights, and perhaps the burning heat of disease, are hinted at as the accompaniments of the soul-agony. It is possible that similar allusions to actual bodily illness are to be found in another psalm, probably referring to the same period, and presenting striking parallelisms of expression (Ps. vi.), "Have mercy upon me, Jehovah, for I languish (fade away); heal me, for my bones are affrighted. My soul is also sore vexed. I am weary with my groaning; every night make I my bed to swim. I water my couch with my tears." The similar phrase, too, in psalm fifty-one, "The bones which Thou hast broken," may have a similar application. Thus, sick in body and soul, he dragged through a weary year—ashamed of his guilty dalliance, wretched in his self-accusations, afraid of God, and skulking in the recesses of his palace from the sight of his people. A goodly price he had sold integrity for. The bread had been sweet for a moment, but how quickly his "mouth is filled with gravel" (Proverbs xx. 17). David learned, what we all learn (and the holier a man is, the more speedily and sharply does the lesson follow on the heels of his sin), that every transgression is a blunder, that we never get the satisfaction which we expect from any sin, or if we do, we get something with it which spoils it all. A nauseous drug is added to the exciting, intoxicating drink which temptation offers, and though its flavour is at first disguised by the pleasanter taste of the sin, its bitterness is persistent though slow, and clings to the palate long after that has faded utterly.

Into this dreary life Nathan's message comes with merciful rebuke. The prompt severity of David's judgment against the selfish sinner of the inimitable apologue may be a subtle indication of his troubled conscience, which fancies some atonement for his own sin in stern repression of that of others; for consciousness of evil may sometimes sting into harshness as well as soften to lenity, and sinful man is a sterner judge than the righteous God. The answer of Nathan is a perfect example of the Divine way of convincing of sin. There is first the plain charge pressed home on the individual conscience, "Thou art the man." Then follows, not reproach nor further deepening of the blackness of the deed, but a tender enumeration of God's great benefits, whereon is built the solemn question, "Wherefore hast thou despised the commandment of the Lord, to do evil in His sight?" The contemplation of God's faithful love, and of the all-sufficient gifts which it bestows, makes every transgression irrational as well as ungrateful, and turns remorse, which consumes like the hot wind of the wilderness, into tearful repentance which refreshes the soul. When God has been seen loving and bestowing ere He commands and requires, it is profitable to hold the image of the man's evil in all its ugliness close up to his eyes; and so the bald facts are repeated next in the fewest, strongest words. Nor can the message close until a rigid law of retribution has been proclaimed, the slow operation of which will filter bitterness and shame through all his life. "And David said unto Nathan, I have sinned against the Lord." Two words (in the Hebrew) make the transition from sullen misery to real though shaded peace. No lengthened outpouring, no accumulation of self-reproach; he is too deeply moved for many words, which he knows God does not need. More would have been less. All is contained in that one sob, in which the whole frostwork of these weary months breaks up and rolls away, swept before the strong flood. And as brief and simple as the confession, is the response, "And Nathan said unto David, The Lord also hath put away thy sin." How full and unconditional the blessing bestowed in these few words; how swift and sufficient the answer! So the long estrangement is ended. Thus simple and Divine is the manner of pardon. In such short compass may the turning point of a life lie! But while confession and forgiveness heal the breach between God and David, pardon is not impunity, and the same sentence which bestows the remission of sin announces the exaction of a penalty. The judgments threatened a moment before—

a moment so far removed now to David's consciousness that it would look as if an age had passed—are not withdrawn, and another is added, the death of Bathsheba's infant. God loves His servants too well to "suffer sin upon them," and the freest forgiveness and the happiest consciousness of it may consist with the loving infliction and the submissive bearing of pains, which are no longer the strokes of an avenging judge, but the chastisements of a gracious father.

The fifty-first psalm must, we think, be conceived of as following soon after Nathan's mission. There may be echoes of the prophet's stern question, "Wherefore hast thou despised the commandment of the Lord, to do evil in His sight?" and of the confession, "I have sinned against the Lord," in the words, "Against Thee, Thee only have I sinned, and done evil in Thy sight" (ver. 4), though perhaps the expressions are not so peculiar as to make the allusion certain. But, at all events, the penitence and prayers of the psalm can scarcely be supposed to have preceded the date of the historical narrative, which clearly implies that the rebuke of the seer was the first thing that broke up the dumb misery of unrepented sin.

Although the psalm is one long cry for pardon and restoration, one can discern an order and progress in its petitions—the order, not of an artificial reproduction of a past mood of mind, but the instinctive order in which the emotion of contrite desire will ever pour itself forth. In the psalm all begins, as all begins in fact, with the grounding of the cry for favour on "Thy loving-kindness," "the multitude of Thy tender mercies;" the one plea that avails with God, whose love is its own motive and its own measure, whose past acts are the standard for all His future, whose compassions, in their innumerable numbers, are more than the sum of our transgressions, though these be "more than the hairs of our head." Beginning with God's mercy, the penitent soul can learn to look next upon its own sin in all its aspects of evil. The depth and intensity of the psalmist's loathing of self is wonderfully expressed in his words for his crime. He speaks of his "transgressions" and of his "sin." Looked at in one way, he sees the separate acts of which he had been guilty —lust, fraud, treachery, murder: looked at in another, he sees them all knotted together, in one inextricable tangle of forked, hissing tongues, like the serpent locks that coil and twist round a Gorgon head. No sin dwells alone; the separate acts have a common root, and the whole is matted together like the green growth on a stagnant pond, so that, by whatever filament it is grasped, the whole mass is drawn towards you. And a profound insight into the essence and character of sin lies in the accumulated synonyms. It is "transgression," or, as the word might be rendered, "rebellion"—not the mere breach of an impersonal law, not merely an infraction of "the constitution of our nature"—but the rising of a subject will against its true king, disobedience to a person as well as contravention of a standard. It is "iniquity"—perversion or distortion—a word which expresses the same metaphor as is found in many languages, namely, crookedness as descriptive of deeds which depart from the perfect line of right. It is "sin," *i.e.*, "missing one's aim;" in which profound word is contained the truth that all sin is a blunder, shooting wide of the true goal, if regard be had to the end of our being, and not less wide if regard be had to our happiness. It ever misses the mark; and the epitaph might be written over every sinner who seeks pleasure at the price of righteousness, " Thou fool."

Nor less pregnant with meaning is the psalmist's emphatic acknowledgment, "Against Thee, Thee only have I sinned." He is not content with looking upon his evil in itself, or in relation only to the people who had suffered by it; he thinks of it in relation to God. He had been guilty of crimes against Bathsheba and Uriah, and even the rough soldier whom he made his tool, as well as against his whole subjects; but, dark as these were, they assumed their true character only when they were discerned as done against God. "Sin," in its full sense, implies "God" as its correlative. We transgress against each other, but we sin against Him.

Nor does the psalmist stop here. He has acknowledged the tangled multiplicity and dreadful unity of his evil, he has seen its inmost character, he has learned to bring his deed into connection with God; what remains still to be confessed? He laments, and that not as extenuation (though it be explanation), but as aggravation, the sinful nature in which he had been born. The deeds had come from a source —a bitter fountain had welled out this blackness.

He himself is evil, therefore he has done evil. The sin is his; he will not contest his full responsibility; and its foul characteristics declare the inward foulness from which it has flowed—and that foulness is himself. Does he therefore think that he is less to blame? By no means. His acknowledgment of an evil nature is the very deepest of his confessions, and leads not to a palliation of his guilt, but to a cry to Him who alone can heal the inward wound; and as He can purge away the transgressions, can likewise stanch their source, and give him to feel within "that he is healed from that plague."

The same intensity of feeling expressed by the use of so many words for sin is revealed also in the reiterated synonyms for pardon. The prayer comes from his lips over and over again, not because he thinks that he shall be heard for his much speaking, but because of the earnestness of his longing. Such repetitions are signs of the persistence of faith, while others, though they last like the prayers of Baal's priests, "from morning till the time of the evening sacrifice," indicate only the suppliant's doubt. David prays that his sins may be "blotted out," in which petition they are conceived as recorded against him in the archives of the heavens; that he may be "washed" from them, in which they are conceived as foul stains upon himself, needing for their removal hard rubbing and beating (for such is, according to some commentators, the force of the word); that he may be "cleansed" —the technical word for the priestly cleansing of the leper, and declaring him clear of the taint. He also, with similar recurrence to the Mosaic symbols, prays that he may be "purged with hyssop." There is a pathetic appropriateness in the petition, for not only lepers, but those who had become defiled by contact with a dead body, were thus purified; and on whom did the taint of corruption cleave as on the murderer of Uriah? The prayer, too, is even more remarkable in the original, which employs a verb formed from the word for "sin;" "and if in our language that were a word in use, it might be translated, 'Thou shalt un-sin me.'"*

In the midst of these abased confessions and cries for pardon there comes with wonderful force and beauty the bold prayer for restoration

* Donne's Sermons, quoted in Perowne, *in. loc.*

to "joy and gladness"—an indication surely of more than ordinary confidence in the full mercy of God, which would efface all the consequences of his sin.

And following upon them are petitions for sanctifying, reiterated and many-sided, like those that have preceded. Three pairs of clauses contain these, in each of which the second member of the clause asks for the infusion into his spirit of some grace from God—that he may possess a "steadfast spirit," "Thy Holy Spirit," "a willing spirit." It is perhaps not an accident that the central petition of the three is the one which most clearly expresses the thought which all imply—that the human spirit can only be renewed and hallowed by the entrance into it of the Divine. We are not to commit the theological anachronism which has been applied with such evil effect to the whole Old Testament, and suppose that David meant by that central clause in his prayer for renewal all that we mean by it; but he meant, at least, that his spiritual nature could be made to love righteousness and hate iniquity by none other power than God's breathing on it. If we may venture to regard this as the heart of the series, the other two on either side of it may be conceived as its consequences. It will then be "a right spirit," or, as the word means, a steadfast spirit, strong to resist, not swept away by surges of passion, nor shaken by terrors of remorse, but calm, tenacious, and resolved, pressing on in the path of holiness, and immovable with the immobility of those who are rooted in God and goodness. It will be a free, or "a willing spirit," ready for all joyful service of thankfulness, and so penetrated with the love of his God that he will delight to do His will, and carry the law charactered in the spontaneous impulses of his renewed nature. Not without profound meaning does the psalmist seem to recur in his hour of penitence to the tragic fate of his predecessor in the monarchy, to whom, as to himself, had been given by the same anointing, the same gift of "the Spirit of God." Remembering how the holy chrism had faded from the raven locks of Saul long before his bloody head had been sent round Philistine cities to glut their revenge, and knowing that if God were "strict to mark iniquity," the gift which had been withdrawn from Saul would not be continued to himself, he prays, not as anointed monarch only, but as sinful man, "Take not Thy Holy Spirit from me." As before he had ventured to ask for the joy of forgiveness, so now he pleads once more for "the joy of Thy salvation," which comes from cleansing, from conscious fellowship—which he had so long and deeply felt, which for so many months had been hid from him by the mists of his own sin. The psalmist's natural buoyancy, the gladness which was an inseparable part of his religion, and had rung from his harp in many an hour of peril, the bold width of his desires, grounded on the clear breadth of his faith in God's perfect forgiveness, are all expressed in such a prayer from such lips at such a time, and may well be pondered and imitated by us.

The lowly prayer which we have been tracing rises ere its close to a vow of renewed praise. It is very beautiful to note how the poet nature, as well as the consciousness of a Divine function, unite in the resolve that crowns the psalm. To David no tribute that he could bring to God seemed so little unworthy—none to himself so joyous—as the music of his harp, and the melody of his songs; nor was any part of his kingly office so lofty in his estimation as his calling to proclaim in glowing words the name of the Lord, that men might learn to love. His earliest song in exile had closed with a like vow. It had been well fulfilled for many a year; but these last doleful months had silenced all his praise. Now, as hope begins to shine upon him once more, the frost which had stilled the stream of his devotion is melting, and as he remembers his glad songs of old, and this miserable dumbness, his final prayer is, "O Lord, open Thou my lips, and my mouth shall show forth Thy praise."

The same consciousness of sin, which we have found in a previous verse discerning the true significance of ceremonial purification, leads also to the recognition of the insufficiency of outward sacrifices—a thought which is not, as some modern critics would fain make it, the product of the latest age of Judaism, but appears occasionally through the whole of the history, and indicates not the date, but the spiritual elevation of its utterer. David sets it on the very summit of his psalm, to sparkle there like some stone of price. The rich jewel which he has brought up from the abyss of degradation is that truth which has shone out from its setting here over three milleniums: "The sacrifices of God are a broken spirit; a broken and a contrite heart, O God, Thou wilt not despise."

The words which follow, containing a prayer for the building up of Zion, and a prediction of the continuous offering of sacrifice, present some difficulty. They do not necessarily presuppose that Jerusalem is in ruins; for "build Thou the walls" would be no less appropriate a petition if the fortifications were unfinished (as we know they were in David's time) than if they had been broken down. Nor do the words contradict the view of sacrifice just given, for the use of the symbol and the conviction of its insufficiency co-existed, in fact, in every devout life, and may well be expressed side by side. But the transition from so intensely personal emotions to intercession for Zion seems almost too sudden even for a nature as wide and warm as David's. If the closing verses are his, we may, indeed, see in them the king re-awaking to a sense of his responsibilities, which he had so long neglected, first, in the selfishness of his heart, and then in the morbid self-absorption of his remorse; and the lesson may be a precious one that the first thought of a pardoned man should be for others. But there is much to be said, on the other hand, in favour of the conjecture that these verses are a later addition, probably after the return from captivity, when the walls of Zion were in ruins, and the altar of the temple had been long cold. If so, then our psalm, as it came from David's full heart, would be all of a piece—one great gush of penitence and faith, beginning with, "Have mercy upon me, O God," ending with the assurance of acceptance, and so remaining for all ages the chart of the thorny and yet blessed path that leads "from death unto life." In that aspect, what it does not contain is as noteworthy as what it does. Not one word asks for exemption from such penalties of his great fall as can be inflicted by a loving Father on a soul that lives in His love. He cries for pardon, but he gives his back to the smiters whom God may please to send.

The other psalm of the penitent (xxxii.) has been already referred to in connection with the autobiographical materials which it contains. It is evidently of a later period than the fifty-first. There is no struggle in it; the prayer has been heard, and this is the beginning of the fulfilment of the vow to show forth God's praise. In the earlier he had said, "Then will I teach transgressors the way;" here he says, "I will instruct thee and teach thee in the way which thou shalt go." There he began with the plaintive cry for mercy; here with a burst of praise celebrating the happiness of the pardoned penitent. There we heard the sobs of a man in the very agony of abasement; here we have the story of their blessed issue. There we had multiplied synonyms for sin, and for the forgiveness which was desired; here it is the many-sided preciousness of forgiveness possessed which runs over in various yet equivalent phrases. There the highest point to which he could climb was the assurance that a bruised heart was accepted, and the bones broken might still rejoice. Here the very first word is of blessedness, and the close summons the righteous to exuberant joy. The one is a psalm of wailing; the other, to use its own words, a "song of deliverance."

What glad consciousness that he himself is the happy man whom he describes rings in the melodious variations of the one thought of forgiveness in the opening words! How gratefully he draws on the treasures of that recent experience, while he sets it forth as being the "taking away" of sin, as if it were the removal of a solid something, or the lifting of a burden off his back; and as the "covering" of sin, as if it were the wrapping of its ugliness in thick folds that hide it for ever even from the all-seeing Eye; and as the "non-reckoning" of sin, as if it were the discharge of a debt! What vivid memory of past misery in the awful portrait of his impenitent self, already referred to — on which the mind dwells in silence, while the musical accompaniment (as directed by the "selah") touches some plaintive minor or grating discord! How noble and eloquent the brief words (echo of the historical narrative) that tell the full and swift forgiveness that followed simple confession — and how effectively the music again comes in, prolonging the thought and rejoicing in the pardon! How sure he is that his experience is of priceless value to the world for all time, when he sees in his absolution a motive that will draw all the godly nearer to their Helper in heaven! How full his heart is of praise, that he cannot but go back again to his own story, and rejoice in God his hiding-place—

whose past wondrous love assures him that in the future songs of deliverance will ring him round, and all his path be encompassed with music of praise.

So ends the more personal part of the psalm. A more didactic portion follows, the generalization of that. Possibly the voice which now speaks is a higher than David's. "I will instruct thee and teach thee in the way which thou shalt go. I will guide thee with mine eye," scarcely sounds like words meant to be understood as spoken by him. They are the promise from heaven of a gentle teaching to the pardoned man, which will instruct by no severity, but by patient schooling; which will direct by no harsh authority, but by that loving glance that is enough for those who love, and is all too subtle and delicate to be perceived by any other. Such gracious direction is not for the psalmist alone, but it needs a spirit in harmony with God to understand it. For others there can be nothing higher than mere force, the discipline of sorrow, the bridle in the hard mouth, the whip for the stiff back. The choice for all men is through penitence and forgiveness to rise to the true position of men, capable of receiving and obeying a spiritual guidance, which appeals to the heart, and gently subdues the will, or by stubborn impenitence to fall to the level of brutes, that can only be held in by a halter and driven by a lash. And because this is the alternative, therefore " Many sorrows shall be to the wicked; but he that trusteth in the Lord, mercy shall compass him about."

And then the psalm ends with a great cry of gladness, three times reiterated, like the voice of a herald on some festal day of a nation: " Rejoice in Jehovah! and leap for joy, O righteous! and gladly shout, all ye upright in heart!"

Such is the end of the sobs of the penitent.

XIV.—CHASTISEMENTS.

THE chastisements, which were the natural fruits of David's sin, soon began to show themselves, though apparently ten years at least passed before Absalom's revolt, at which time he was probably a man of sixty. But these ten years were very weary and sad. There is no more joyous activity, no more conquering energy, no more consciousness of his people's love. Disasters thicken round him, and may all be traced to his great sin. His children learned the lesson it had taught them, and lust and fratricide desolated his family. A parent can have no sharper pang than the sight of his own sins reappearing in his child. David saw the ghastly reflection of his unbridled passion in his eldest son's foul crime (and even a gleam of it in his unhappy daughter), and of his murderous craft in his second son's bloody revenge. Whilst all this hell of crime is boiling round him, a strange passiveness seems to have crept over the king, and to have continued till his flight before Absalom. The narrative is singularly silent about him. He seems paralysed by the consciousness of his past sin; he originates nothing. He dares not punish Ammon; he can only weep when he hears of Absalom's crime. He weakly longs for the return of the latter from his exile, but cannot nerve himself to send for him till Joab urges it. A flash of his old kingliness blazes out for a moment in his refusal to see his son; but even that slight satisfaction to justice vanishes as soon as Joab chooses to insist that Absalom shall return to court. He seems to have no will of his own. He has become a mere tool in the hands of his fierce general—and Joab's hold upon him was his complicity in Uriah's murder. Thus at every step he was dogged by the consequences of his crime, even though it was pardoned sin. And if, as is probable, Ahithophel was Bathsheba's grandfather, the most formidable person in Absalom's conspiracy, whose defection wounded him so deeply, was no doubt driven to the usurper's side out of revenge for the insult to his house in her person. Thus "of our pleasant vices doth heaven make whips to scourge us." "Be not deceived; whatsoever a man soweth, that shall he also reap."

It is not probable that many psalms were made in those dreary days. But the forty-first and fifty-fifth are, with reasonable probability, referred to this period by many commentators. They give a very touching picture of the old king during the four years in which Absalom's conspiracy was being hatched. It seems, from the forty-first, that the pain and sorrow of his heart had brought on some serious illness, which his enemies had used for their own purposes, and embittered by hypocritical condolences and and ill-concealed glee. The sensitive nature of the psalmist winces under their heartless desertion of him, and pours out its plaint in this pathetic lament. He begins with a blessing on those who "consider the afflicted"—having reference, perhaps, to the few who were faithful to him in his languishing sickness. He passes thence to his own case, and, after humble confession of his sin,—almost in the words of the fifty-first psalm,—he tells how his sickbed had been surrounded by very different visitors. His disease drew no pity, but only fierce impatience that he lingered in life so long. "Mine enemies speak evil of me—when will he die, and his name have perished?" One of them, in especial, who must have been a man in high position to gain access to the sick chamber, has been conspicuous by his lying words of condolence: "If he come to see me he speaketh vanity." The sight of the sick king touched no chord of affection, but only increased the traitor's animosity—"his heart gathereth evil to itself"—and then, having watched his pale face for wished-for unfavourable symptoms, the false friend hurries from the bedside to talk of his hopeless illness—"he goeth abroad, he telleth it." The tidings spread, and are stealthily passed from one conspirator to another. "All that hate me whisper together against me." They exaggerate the gravity of his condition, and are glad because, making the wish the father to the thought, they believe him dying. "A thing of Belial" (*i.e.*, a destructive disease), "say they, is poured out upon him, and now that he lieth, he shall rise up no more." And, sharpest pang of all, that among these traitors, and probably the same person as he whose heartless presence in the sick chamber was so hard to bear, should be Ahithophel, whose counsel had been like an oracle from God. Even he, "the man of my friendship, in whom I trusted, which did eat of my bread"—he, like an ignoble, vicious mule—"has lifted high his heel" against the sick lion.

We should be disposed to refer the thirty-ninth psalm also to this period. It, too, is the meditation of one in sickness, which he knows to be a Divine judgment for his sin. There is little trace of enemies in it; but his attitude is that of silent submission, while wicked men are disquieted around him—which is precisely the characteristic peculiarity of his conduct at this period. It consists of two parts (vers. 1—6 and 7—13), in both of which the subjects of his meditations are the same, but the tone of them different. His own sickness and mortality, and man's fleeting, shadowy life, are his themes. The former has led him to think of the latter. The first effect of his sorrow was to close his lips in a silence that was not altogether submission. "I held my peace, even from good, and my sorrow was stirred." As in his sin, when he kept silence, his "bones waxed old," so now in his sorrow and sickness the pain that could not find expression raged the more violently. The tearless eyes were hot and aching; but he conquered the dumb spirit, and could carry his heavy thoughts to God. They are very heavy at first. He only desires that the sad truth may be driven deeper into his soul. With the engrossment so characteristic of melancholy, he asks, what might have been thought the thing he needed least, "Make me to know mine end;" and then he dilates on the gloomy reflections which he had been cherishing in silence. Not only he himself, with his handbreadth of days, that shrink into absolute nothingness when brought into contrast with the life of God, but "every man," even when apparently "standing" most "firm, is only a breath." As a shadow every man moves spectral among shadows. The tumult that fills their lives is madness; "only for a breath are they disquieted." So bitterly, with an anticipation of the sad, clear-eyed pity and scorn of "The Preacher," does the sick and wearied king speak, in tones very unlike the joyous music of his earlier utterances.

But, true and wholesome as such thoughts are, they are not all the truth. So the prayer changes in tone, even while its substance is the same. He rises from the shows of earth to his true home, driven thither by their hollowness. "My hope is in Thee." The conviction of earth's vanity is all different when it has "tossed him to Thy breast." The pardoned sinner, who never thereafter forgot his grievous fall, asks for deliverance "from all his trangressions." The sullen silence has changed into full acquiescence: "I opened not my mouth, because Thou didst it,"—a silence differing from the other as the calm after the storm, when all the winds sleep and the sun shines out on a freshened world, differs from the boding stillness while the slow thunder-clouds grow lurid on the horizon. He cries for healing, for he knows his sickness to be the buffet and assault of God's hand; and its bitterness is assuaged, even while its force continues, by the conviction that it is God's fatherly chastisement for sin which gnaws away his manly vigour as the moth frets his kingly robe. The very thought which had been so bitter—that every man is vanity—reappears in a new connection as the basis of the prayer that God would hear, and is modified so as to become infinitely blessed and hopeful. "I am a stranger with Thee, and a sojourner, as all my fathers were." A wanderer indeed, and a transient guest on earth; but what of that, if he be God's guest? All that is sorrowful is drawn off from the thought when we realise our connection with God. We are in God's house; the host, not the guest, is responsible for the housekeeping. We need not feel life lonely if He be with us, nor its shortness sad. It is not a shadow, a dream, a breath, if it be rooted in Him. And thus the sick man has conquered his gloomy thoughts, even though he sees little before him but the end; and he is not cast down even though his desires are all summed up in one for a little respite and healing, ere the brief trouble of earth be done with: "O spare me, that I may recover strength before I go hence, and be no more."

It may be observed that this supposition of a protracted illness, which is based upon these psalms, throws light upon the singular passiveness of David during the maturing of Absalom's conspiracy, and may naturally be supposed to have favoured his schemes, an essential part of which was to ingratiate himself with suitors who came to the king for judgment by affecting great regret that no man was deputed of the king to hear them. The accumulation of untried causes, and the apparent disorganization of the judicial machinery, are well accounted for by David's sickness.

The fifty-fifth psalm gives some very pathetic additional particulars. It is in three parts—a plaintive prayer and portraiture of the psalmist's mental distress (vers. 1—8); a vehement supplication against his foes, and indignant recounting of their treachery (vers. 9—16); and, finally, a prophecy of the retribution that is to fall upon them (vers. 17—23). In the first and second portions we have some points which help to complete our picture of the man. For instance, his heart "writhes" within him, the "terrors of death" are on him, "fear and trembling" are come on him, and "horror" has covered him. All this points, like subsequent verses, to his knowledge of the conspiracy before it came to a head. The state of the city, which is practically in the hands of Absalom and his tools, is described with bold imagery. Violence and Strife in possession of it, spies prowling about the walls day and night, Evil and Trouble in its midst, and Destruction, Oppression, and Deceit—a goodly company—flaunting in its open spaces. And the spirit, the brain of the whole, is the trusted friend whom he had made his own equal, who had shared his secretest thoughts in private, who had walked next him in solemn processions to the temple. Seeing all this, what does the king do, who was once so fertile in resource, so decisive in counsel, so prompt in action? Nothing. His only weapon is prayer. "As for me, I will call upon God; and the Lord will save me. Evening, and morning, and at noon, will I pray, and cry aloud: and He shall hear my voice." He lets it all grow as it list, and only longs to be out of all the weary coil of troubles. "Oh that I had wings like a dove, then would I fly away and be at rest. Lo, I would flee far off, I would lodge in the wilderness. I would swiftly fly to my refuge from the raging wind, from the tempest." The langour of his disease, love for his worthless son, consciousness of sin, and submission to the chastisement through "one of his own house," which Nathan had foretold, kept him quiet, though he saw the plot winding its meshes round him. And in this submission patient confidence is not wanting, though subdued and saddened, which finds expression in the last words of this psalm of the heavy laden, "Cast thy burden upon Jehovah.

He, He will sustain thee. . . . I will trust in Thee."

When the blow at last fell, the same passive acquiescence in what he felt to be God's chastisement is very noticeable. Absalom escapes to Hebron, and sets up the standard of revolt. When the news comes to Jerusalem the king's only thought is immediate flight. He is almost cowardly in his eagerness to escape, and is prepared to give up everything without a blow. It seems as if only a touch was needed to overthrow his throne. He hurries on the preparations for flight with nervous haste. He forms no plans beyond those of his earlier wish to fly away and be at rest. He tries to denude himself of followers. When the six hundred men of Gath—who had been with him ever since his early days in Philistia, and had grown grey in his service—make themselves the van of his little army, he urges the heroic Ittai, their leader, to leave him a fugitive, and to worship the rising sun, "Return to thy place, and abide with *the king*"—so thoroughly does he regard the crown as passed already from his brows. The priests with the ark are sent back; he is not worthy to have the symbol of the Divine presence identified with his doubtful cause, and is prepared to submit without a murmur if God "thus say, I have no delight in thee." With covered head and naked feet he goes up the slope of Olivet, and turning perhaps at that same bend in the rocky mountain path where the true King, coming to the city, wept as he saw its shining walls and soaring pinnacles across the narrow valley, the discrowned king and all his followers broke into passionate weeping as they gazed their last on the lost capital, and then with choking sobs rounded the shoulder of the hill and set their faces to their forlorn flight. Passing through the territory of Saul's tribe—dangerous ground for him to tread—the rank hatred of Shimei's heart blossoms into speech. With Eastern vehemence, he curses and flings stones and dust in the transports of his fury, stumbling along among the rocks high up on the side of the glen, as he keeps abreast of the little band below. Did David remember how the husband from whom he had torn Michal had followed her to this very place, and there had turned back weeping to his lonely home? The remembrance, at any rate, of later and more evil deeds prompted his meek answer, "Let him curse, for the Lord hath bidden him."

The first force of the disaster spent itself, and by the time he was safe across Jordan, on the free uplands of Bashan, his spirit rises. He makes a stand at Mahanaim, the place where his great ancestor, in circumstances somewhat analogous to his own, had seen the vision of "bright-harnessed angels" ranked in battle array for the defence of himself and his own little band, and called the name of the place the "two camps." Perhaps that old story helped to hearten him, as the defection of Ahithophel from the conspiracy certainly would do. As the time went on, too, it became increasingly obvious that the leaders of the rebellion were "infirm of purpose," and that every day of respite from actual fighting diminished their chances of success, as that politic adviser saw so plainly. Whatever may have been the reason, it is clear that by the time David had reached Mahanaim he had resolved not to yield without a struggle. He girds on his sword once more with some of the animation of early days, and the light of trustful valour blazes again in his old eyes.

XV.—THE SONGS OF THE FUGITIVE.

THE psalms which probably belong to the period of Absalom's rebellion correspond well with the impression of his spirit gathered from the historical books. Confidence in God, submission to His will, are strongly expressed in them, and we may almost discern a progress in the former respect as the rebellion grows. They flame brighter and brighter in the deepening darkness. From the lowest abyss the stars are seen most clearly. He is far more buoyant when he is an exile once more in the wilderness, and when the masks of plot and trickery are fallen, and the danger stands clear before him. Like some good ship issuing from the shelter of the pier heads, the first blow of the waves throws her over on her side and makes her quiver like a living thing recoiling from a terror, but she rises above the tossing surges and keeps her course. We may allocate with a fair amount of likelihood the following psalms to this period

—iii.; iv.; xxv. (?); xxviii. (?); lviii. (?); lxi.; lxii.; lxiii.; cix. (?); cxliii.

The first two of these form a pair; they are a morning and an evening hymn. The little band are encamped on their road to Mahanaim, with no roof but the stars, and no walls but the arm of God. In the former the discrowned king sings, as he rises from his nightly bivouac. He pours out first his plaint of the foes, who are described as "many," and as saying that, "There is no help for him in God," words which fully correspond to the formidable dimensions of the revolt, and to the belief which actuated the conspirators, and had appeared as possible even to himself, that his sin had turned away the aid of heaven from his cause. To such utterances of malice and confident hatred he opposes the conviction which had again filled his soul, that even in the midst of real peril and the shock of battle Jehovah is his "shield." With bowed and covered head he had fled from Jerusalem, but "Thou art the lifter up of mine head." He was an exile from the tabernacle on Zion, and he had sent back the ark to its rest; but though he has to cry to God from beyond Jordan, He answers "from His holy hill."

He and his men camped amidst dangers, but one unslumbering Helper mounted guard over their undefended slumbers. "I laid me down and slept" there among the echoes of the hills. "I awaked, for Jehovah sustained me;" and another night has passed without the sudden shout of the rebels breaking the silence, or the gleam of their swords in the starlight. The experience of protection thus far heartens him to front even the threatening circle of his foes around him, whom it is his pain to think of as "the people" of God, and yet as his foes. And then he betakes himself in renewed energy of faith to his one weapon of prayer, and even before the battle sees the victory, and the Divine power fracturing the jaws and breaking the teeth of the wild beasts who hunt him. But his last thought is not of retribution nor of fear; for himself he rises to the height of serene trust, "Salvation is of the Lord;" and for his foes and for all the nation that had risen against him his thoughts are worthy of a true king, freed from all personal animosity, and his words are a prayer conceived in the spirit of Him whose dying breath was intercession for His rebellious subjects who crucified their King, "Thy blessing be upon Thy people."

The fourth psalm is the companion evening hymn. Its former portion (vers. 2—4) seems to be a remonstrance addressed as if to the leaders of the revolt ("sons of men" being equivalent to "persons of rank and dignity"). It is the expression in vivid form, most natural to such a nature, of his painful feeling under their slanders; and also of his hopes and desires for them, that calm thought in these still evening hours which are falling on the world may lead them to purer service and to reliance on God. So forgivingly, so lovingly does he think of them, ere he lays himself down to rest, wishing that "on their beds," as on his, the peace of meditative contemplation may rest, and the day of war's alarms be shut in by holy "communion with their own hearts" and with God.

The second portion turns to himself and his followers, among whom we may suppose some faint hearts were beginning to despond; and to them, as to the very enemy, David would fain be the bringer of a better mind. "Many say, Who will show us good?" He will turn them from their vain search round the horizon on a level with their own eyes for the appearance of succour. They must look upwards, not round about. They must turn their question, which only expects a negative answer, into a prayer, fashioned like that triple priestly benediction of old (Numbers vi. 24—26). His own experience bursts forth irrepressible. He had prayed in his hour of penitence, "Make me to hear joy and gladness" (Psa. li.); and the prayer had been answered, if not before, yet now when peril had brought him nearer to God, and trust had drawn God nearer to him. In his calamity, as is ever the case with devout souls, his joy increased, as Greek fire burns more brightly under water. Therefore this pauper sovereign, discrowned and fed by the charity of the Gileadite pastoral chief, sings, "Thou hast put gladness in my heart, more than in the time that their corn and wine increased." And how tranquilly the psalm closes, and seems to lull itself to rest, "In peace I will at once lie down and sleep, for Thou, O Jehovah, only makest me dwell safely." The growing security which experience of God's care should ever bring, is beautifully marked by the variation on the similar phrase in the previous psalm. There he gratefully recorded that he had laid himself down and slept; here he promises himself that he will lie down "in peace;" and not only so, but that at once on his lying down he will sleep—kept awake by no anxieties, by no bitter thoughts, but, homeless and in danger as he is, will close his eyes, like a tired child, without a care or a fear, and forthwith sleep, with the pressure and the protection of his Father's arm about him.

This psalm sounds again the glad trustful strain which has slumbered in his harp-strings ever since the happy old days of his early trials, and is re-awakened as the rude blast of calamity sweeps through them once more.

The sixty-third psalm is by the superscription referred to the time when David was "in the wilderness of Judah," which has led many readers to think of his long stay there during Saul's persecution. But the psalm certainly belongs to the period of his reign, as is obvious from its words, "*The king* shall rejoice in God." It must therefore belong to his brief sojourn in the same wilderness on his flight to Mahanaim, when, as we read in 2 Sam., "The people were weary and hungry and thirsty in the wilderness." There is a beautiful progress of thought in it, which is very obvious if we notice the triple occurrence of the words "my soul," and their various connections—"my soul thirsteth," "my soul is satisfied," "my soul followeth hard after Thee;" or, in other words, the psalm is a transcript of the passage of a believing soul from longing through fruition to firm trust, in which it is sustained by the right hand of God.

The first of these emotions, which is so natural to the fugitive in his sorrows, is expressed with singular poetic beauty in language borrowed from the ashen grey monotony of the waterless land in which he was. One of our most accurate and least imaginative travellers describes it thus: "There were no signs of vegetation, with the exception of a few reeds and rushes, and here and there a tamarisk." This lonely land, cracked with drought, as if gaping with chapped lips for the rain that comes not, is the image of his painful yearning for the Fountain of living waters. As his men plodded along over the burning marl, fainting for thirst and finding nothing in the dry torrent beds, so he longed for the refreshment of that gracious presence. Then he remembers how in happier days he had had the same desires, and they had been satisfied in the tabernacle. Probably the words should read, "Thus in the sanctuary have I gazed upon Thee, to see Thy power and Thy glory." In the desert and in the sanctuary his longing had been the same, but then he had been able to behold the symbol which bore the name, "the glory,"—and now he wanders far from it. How beautifully this regretful sense of absence from and pining after the ark is illustrated by those inimitably pathetic words of the fugitive's answer to the priests who desired to share his exile. "And the king said unto Zadok, Carry back the ark of God into the city. If I find favour in the eyes of the Lord, He will bring me again, and show me both it and His habitation."

The fulfilment is cotemporaneous with the desire. The swiftness of the answer is beautifully indicated in the quick turn with which the psalm passes from plaintive longing to exuberant rapture of fruition. In the one breath "my soul thirsteth;" in the next, "my soul is satisfied"—as when in tropical lands the rain comes, and in a day or two what had been baked earth is rich meadow, and the dry torrent-beds, where the white stones glistered in the sunshine, foam with rushing waters and are edged with budding willows. The fulness of satisfaction when God fills the soul is vividly expressed in the familiar image of the feast of "marrow and fatness," on which he banquets even while hungry in the desert. The abundant delights of fellowship with God make him insensible to external privations, are drink for him thirsty, food for his hunger, a home in his wanderings, a source of joy and music in the midst of much that is depressing: "My mouth shall praise Thee with joyful lips." The little camp had to keep keen look-out for nightly attacks; and it is a slight link of connection, very natural under the circumstances, between the psalms of this period, that they all have some references to the perilous hours of darkness. We have found him laying himself down to sleep in peace; here he wakes, not to guard from hostile surprises, but in the silence there below the stars to think of God and feel again the fulness of His all-sufficiency. Happy thoughts, not fears, hold His eyes waking. "I remember Thee upon my bed."

The fruition heartens for renewed exercise of

confidence, in which David feels himself upheld by God, and foresees his enemies' defeat and his own triumph. "My soul cleaveth after Thee"—a remarkable phrase, in which the two metaphors of tenacious adherence and eager following are mingled to express the two "phases of faith," which are really one—of union with and quest after God, the possession which pursues, the pursuit which possesses Him who is at once grasped and felt after by the finite creature whose straitest narrowness is not too narrow to be blessed by some indwelling of God, but whose widest expansion of capacity and desire can but contain a fragment of His fulness. From such elevation of high communion he looks down and onward into the dim future, his enemies sunken, like Korah and his rebels, into the gaping earth, or scattered in fight, and the jackals that were snuffing hungrily about his camp in the wilderness gorging themselves on corpses, while he himself, once more "king," shall rejoice in God, and with his faithful companions, whose lips and hearts were true to God and His anointed, shall glory in the deliverance that by the arbitrament of victory has flung back the slanders of the rebels in their teeth, and choked them with their own lies.

Our space forbids more than a brief reference to psalm lxii., which seems also to belong to this time. It has several points of contact with those already considered, *e.g.*, the phrase, "sons of men," in the sense of "nobles" (ver. 9); "my soul," as equivalent to "myself," and yet as a kind of quasi-separate personality which he can study and exhort; the significant use of the term "people," and the double exhortations to his own devout followers and to the arrogant enemy. The whole tone is that of patient resignation, which we have found characterising David now. The first words are the key-note of the whole, "Truly unto God my soul is silence"—is all one great stillness of submissive waiting upon Him. It was in the very crisis of his fate, in the suspense of the uncertain issue of the rebellion, that these words, the very sound of which has calmed many a heart since, welled to his lips. The expression of unwavering faith and unbroken peace is much heightened by the frequent recurrence of the word which is variously translated "truly," "surely," and "only." It carries the force of confident affirmation, like the "verily" of the New Testament, and is here most significantly prefixed to the assertions of his patient resignation (ver. 1); of God's defence (ver. 2); of the enemies' whispered counsels (ver. 4); to his exhortation of his soul to the resignation which it already exercises (ver. 5); and to the triumphant reiteration of God's all-sufficient protection. How beautifully, too, does that reiteration—almost verbal repetition—of the opening words strengthen the impression of his habitual trust. His soul in its silence murmurs to itself, as it were, the blessed thoughts over and over again. Their echoes haunt his spirit "lingering and wandering on, as loth to die;" and if for a moment the vision of his enemies disturbs their flow, one indignant question flung at them suffices, "How long will ye rush upon a man? (how long) will ye all of you thrust him down as (if he were) a bowing wall, a tottering fence?" and with a rapid glance at their plots and bitter words, he comes back again to his calm gaze on God. Lovingly he accumulates happy names for Him, which, in their imagery, as well as in their repetition, remind us of the former songs of the fugitive.

"My rock," in whom I hide; "He is my salvation," which is even more than "from Him cometh my salvation;" my "fortress," my "glory," "the rock of my strength," "my refuge." So many phases of his need and of God's sufficiency thus gathered together, tell how familiar to the thoughts and real to the experience of the aged fugitive was his security in Jehovah, The thirty years since last he had wandered there have confirmed the faith of his earlier songs; and though the ruddy locks of the young chieftain are silvered with grey now, and sins and sorrows have saddened him, yet he can take up again with deeper meaning the tones of his old praise, and let the experience of age seal with its "verily" the hopes of youth. Exhortations to his people to unite themselves with him in his faith, and assurances that God is a refuge for them too, with solemn warnings to the rebels, close this psalm of glad submission. It is remarkable for the absence of all petitions. He needs nothing beyond what he has. As the companion psalm says, his soul "is satisfied." Communion with God has its moments of restful blessedness, when desire is stilled, and expires in peaceful fruition.

The other psalms of this period must be unnoticed. The same general tone pervades them all. In many particulars they closely resemble those of the Sauline period. But the resemblance fails very significantly at one point. The emphatic assertion of his innocence is gone for ever. Pardoned indeed he is, cleansed, conscious of God's favour, and able to rejoice in it; but carrying to the end the remembrance of his sore fall, and feeling it all the more penitently, the more he is sure of God's forgiveness. Let us remember that there are sins which, once done, leave their traces on memory and conscience, painting indelible forms on the walls of our "chambers of imagery," and transmitting results which remission and sanctifying do not, on earth at least, wholly obliterate. Let David's youthful prayer be ours, "Keep back Thy servant from presumptuous sins: then shall I be upright, and I shall be innocent from much transgression."

It does not fall within the scope of this volume to deal with the suppression of Absalom's revolt, nor with the ten years of rule that remained to David after his restoration. The psalter does not appear to contain psalms which throw light upon the somewhat clouded closing years of his reign. One psalm, indeed, there is attributed to him, which is, at any rate, the work of an old man—a sweet song into which mellow wisdom has condensed its final lessons —and a snatch of it may stand instead of any summing-up of the life by us:

> "Trust in the Lord, and do good;
> Dwell in the land, and enjoy security;
> Delight thyself also in the Lord,
> And He shall give thee the desires of thy heart.
> Commit thy way unto the Lord.
>
> Rest in the Lord and wait patiently for Him.
>
> I have been young and now am old,
> Yet have I not seen the righteous forsaken.
>
> I have seen the wicked in great power,
> And spreading himself like a green tree. . . .
> Yet he passed away, and, lo, he was not."

May we not apply the next words to the psalmist himself, and hear him calling us to look on him as he lies on his dying bed—disturbed though it were by ignoble intrigues of hungry heirs—after so many storms nearing the port; after so many vicissitudes, close to the unchanging home; after so many struggles, resting quietly on the breast of God: "Mark the perfect man, and behold the upright, for the end of that man is peace?" Into this opal calmness, as of the liquid light of sunset, all the flaming splendours of the hot day have melted. The music of his songs die away into "peace;" as when some master holds our ears captive with tones so faint that we scarce can tell sound from silence, until the jar of common noises, which that low sweetness had deadened, rushes in.

One strain of a higher mood is preserved for us in the historical books that prophesy of the true King, whom his own failures and sins, no less than his consecration and victories, had taught him to expect. The dying eyes see on the horizon of the far-off future the form of Him who is to be a just and perfect ruler; before the brightness of whose presence, and the refreshing of whose influence, verdure and beauty shall clothe the world. As the shades gather, that radiant glory to come brightens. He departs in peace, having seen the salvation from afar. It was fitting that this fullest of his prophecies should be the last of his strains, as if the rapture which thrilled the trembling strings had snapped them in twain.

And then, for earth, the richest voice which

God ever tuned for His praise was hushed, and the harp of Jesse's son hangs untouched above his grave. But for him death was God's last, best answer to his prayer, "O Lord, open Thou my lips;" and as that cold but most loving hand unclothes him from the weakness of flesh, and leads him in among the choirs of heaven, we can almost hear again his former thanksgiving breaking from his immortal lips, "Thou hast put a new song into my mouth," whose melodies, unsaddened by plaintive minors of penitence and pain, are yet nobler and sweeter than the psalms which he sang here, and left to be the solace and treasure of all generations!

INDEX.

PSALM	PAGE	PSALM	PAGE
iii.	246	xxxiv.	86
iv.	248	xxxv.	139
vii.	110	xxxvii.	259
viii.	28	xxxix.	236
xi.	138	xli.	234
xiii.	138	li.	209
xv.	177	lii.	72
xvii.	138	liv.	100
xviii.	153 and 157	lv.	240
xix.	24	lvi.	77
xx.	203	lvii.	119
xxii.	141	lix.	63
xxiii.	37	lx.	201
xxiv.	177	lxii.	255
xxv.	138	lxiii.	250
xxvii.	89	lxiv.	138
xxix.	31	lxviii.	208
xxxi.	132	cx.	189
xxxii.	227	cxliii.	128

www.ingramcontent.com/pod-product-compliance
Lightning Source LLC
Chambersburg PA
CBHW032002230426
43672CB00010B/2244